Estate Planning Essentials

A Special Request

Your brief Amazon review could really helps us!
The link below will take you to the Amazon.com review page for this book. Please leave a review.

www.estate-bee.com/review6

EstateBee

By EstateBee Publishing

Bibliographic Data

- International Standard Book Number (ISBN): 978-1-913889-16-6
- Printed in the United States of America
- First Edition: December 2010
- Second Edition: January 2013
- Third Edition: January 2014
- Fourth Edition: December 2020 (Updated January 2025)

Published By:

EstateBee Limited
33 Canonbie Road
London SE23 3AW
United Kingdom

Printed and Distributed By: Kindle Direct Publishing, an Amazon Company

For more information, e-mail books@estate-bee.com.

Important Note

This book is meant as a general guide to preparing an estate plan. While effort has been made to make this book as accurate as possible, laws and their interpretation are constantly changing. As such, you are advised to update this information with your own research and/or counsel and to consult with your personal legal, financial, and/or medical advisors before acting on any information contained in this book.

The purpose of this book is to educate and entertain. It is not meant to provide legal, financial, or medical advice or to create any attorney-client or other advisory relationship. The authors and publisher shall have neither liability (whether in negligence or otherwise) nor responsibility to any person or entity with respect to any loss or damage caused or alleged to be caused directly or indirectly by the information contained in this book or the use of that information.

About EstateBee

EstateBee, the international self-help legal publisher, was founded in 2000 by lawyers from one of the most prestigious international law firms in the World.

Our aim was simple - to provide access to quality legal information and products at an affordable price.

Our will writing software was first published in that year and, following its adaptation to cater for the legal systems of various countries worldwide, quickly drew more than 40,000 visitors per month to our website. From this humble start, EstateBee has quickly grown to become a leading international estate planning and asset protection self-help publisher with legal titles in the United States, Canada, the United Kingdom, Australia, and Ireland.

Our publications provide customers with the confidence and knowledge to help them deal with everyday estate planning issues such as the preparation of a last will and testament, a living trust, a power of attorney, administering an estate and much more.

By providing customers with much needed information and forms, we enable them to place themselves in a position where they can protect both themselves and their families using easy to read legal documents and forward planning techniques.

The Future....

We are always seeking to expand and improve the products and services we offer. However, to do this, we need to hear from interested authors and to receive feedback from our customers.

If something is not clear to you in one of our publications, please let us know and we will try to make it clearer in the next edition. If you cannot find the answer you want and have a suggestion for an addition to our range, we will happily look at that too.

Using Self-Help Books

Before using a self-help book, you need to carefully consider the advantages and disadvantages of doing so – particularly where the subject matter is of a legal or tax related nature.

In writing our self-help books, we try to provide readers with an overview of the laws in a specific area, as well as some sample documents. While this overview is often general in nature, it provides a good starting point for those wishing to carry out a more detailed review of a topic.

However, unlike an attorney advising a client, we cannot cover every conceivable eventuality that might affect our readers. Within the intended scope of this book, we can only cover the principal areas in each topic, and even where we cover these areas, we can still only do so to a moderate extent. To do otherwise would result in the writing of a textbook which would be capable of use by legal professionals. This is not what we do.

We try to present useful information and documents that can be used by an average reader with little or no legal knowledge. While our sample documents can be used in most cases, everybody's personal circumstances are different. As such, they may not be suitable for everyone. You may have personal circumstances which might impact the effectiveness of these documents or even your desire to use them. The reality is that without engaging an attorney to review your personal circumstances, this risk will always exist. It's for this very reason that you need to consider whether the cost of using a do-it-yourself legal document outweighs the risk that there may be something special about your particular circumstances which might not be taken into account by the sample documents attached to this book (or indeed any other sample documents).

It goes without saying (we hope) that if you are in any doubt as to whether the documents in this book are suitable for use in your particular circumstances, you should contact a suitably qualified attorney for advice before using them. Remember the decision to use these documents is yours. We are not advising you in any respect.

In using this book, you should also consider the fact that this book has been written with the purpose of providing a general overview of the laws in the United States. As such, it does not attempt to cover all the various procedural nuances and specific requirements that may apply from state to state – although we do point some of these out along the way. Rather, in our book, we try to provide forms which give a fair example of the type of forms which are commonly used in most states. Nevertheless, it remains possible that your state may have specific requirements which have not been considered in our forms.

Another thing that you should remember is that the law changes – thousands of new laws are brought into force every day and, by the same token, thousands are repealed or amended every day. As such, it is possible that while you are reading this book, the law might well have been changed. We hope it has not, but the chance does exist. To address this, when we become aware of them, we do send updates to our customers about material changes to the law. We also ensure that our books are reviewed and revised regularly to take account of these changes.

Anyway, assuming that all the above is acceptable to you, let us move on to exploring the topic at hand.........estate planning.

Table of Contents

CHAPTER 3
Gifts and Beneficiaries 53

CHAPTER 5
Executors & Probate 97

CHAPTER 8
Probate Avoidance Measures 143

CHAPTER 14
Digital Estate Planning 217

CHAPTER 15
Finalizing Your Plan. 223

Appendix 1 233

An Introduction to Estate Planning

Despite the onslaught of estate planning books coming on the market over the last few years, many people remain only vaguely familiar with the subject. In fact, most still believe that estate planning is as simple as making a will. Unsurprisingly, there is a little more to it than that.

Estate planning is the process of (i) arranging for the future management of your affairs in the event that you become incapacitated and (ii) arranging your affairs to maximize the value of your estate that will pass to your beneficiaries following your death.

Important Note

The value of your estate is equal to the value of your total assets (i.e. all your legal rights, interests, and entitlements to property of any kind) less your total liabilities.

Devices such as trusts, powers of attorney and living wills are commonly used for the purpose of providing for the management of a person's affairs at a time when they are no longer able to do so; while devices such as wills and living trusts are used to transfer assets to designated beneficiaries on death. In addition to these devices, there are many others which can be used to transfer, protect, and manage a person's estate.

By using these devices, you will be able to determine:

- How and by whom your assets will be managed during any period in which you are incapacitated and unable to manage your affairs.

- How healthcare decisions will be made during any period in which you are incapacitated and unable to make those decisions yourself.

- When and under what circumstances (if any) your assets will be distributed during your lifetime.

- How and to whom your assets will be distributed following your death.

With a few exceptions, the way you choose to manage and dispose of your estate is entirely up to you. Of course, your choices will to a large extent be dictated by your personal circumstances as well as your priorities and preferences in life. For example, if you are married and have children, you will most likely want to provide for your family following your death. However, if you are separated or divorced, you may wish to disinherit your spouse or ex-spouse completely. Similarly, if you have fallen out with a child you may want to disinherit him or her in favor of someone else.

When it comes to managing your financial or medical affairs during periods of incapacity, you may feel that family members are not up to the challenge. You may even prefer to keep your personal affairs secret from them. In such instances, you may choose to delegate management and decision-making responsibilities to a trusted friend or colleague. Everyone will have their own unique reasons for the decisions they make – and you will be no different.

Did You Know

By now, you've no doubt heard the story of Warren Buffet, the billionaire investor (worth an estimated $117 billion in January 2025 according to Forbes Magazine) who announced that he planned to give away much of his fortune to charity, with 83 percent of it allegedly going to the Bill & Melinda Gates Foundation. Or what about the multi-millionaire founder of The Body Shop, Dame Anita Roddick? She died in 2007 at the age of 64, leaving her entire estate to charity— and her two daughters without a single red cent on "moral grounds."

Your unique circumstances and beliefs are the very reasons you should carefully consider and plan for the distribution of your estate after your death. If you do not take the time to make these decisions yourself, the law will make them for you.

In this book, we introduce you to some of the ways in which you can plan your estate. We talk to you about wills, trusts, powers of attorneys, healthcare directives, beneficiaries, taxes and much more. By the end of this book, not only will you have a solid understanding of estate planning and the techniques involved, but you will also have a firm understanding of why you need to have an estate plan. With a little luck, we will also have inspired you to make an estate plan and have convinced you that it is not nearly as difficult as you may have imagined. While everyone's situation is different, the reality is that most people can prepare an estate plan without needing to involve a lawyer. There are some areas where legal assistance can be beneficial, and we will flag these along the way.

For now, let us start by looking at what estate planning is all about.

CHAPTER 1

Estate Planning Basics

What is Estate Planning?

As mentioned in the introduction, estate planning is the process of arranging for the management of your estate during incapacity, providing for the disposition of your assets upon your death, and maximizing the value of the assets passing to your beneficiaries. It is also the process by which you arrange for the making of healthcare decisions if you become incapacitated before death.

Preparing an estate plan is the most important step you can take to ensure your healthcare wishes are honored if you become incapacitated, and that your intentions regarding the transfer of your property upon death are complied with.

While people traditionally believed that having a will amounted to having an estate plan, more and more people now appreciate the value of having a comprehensive estate plan. Such a plan includes relevant legal devices to transfer property, appoint guardians for children, reduce taxes, avoid probate, provide for the management of financial affairs during times of incapacity, and to appoint agents to make healthcare decisions. A good estate plan should also contain details regarding funeral and burial arrangements. Irrespective of a person's age or the size of their estate, an estate plan can accomplish each of these tasks.

For most people, understanding estate planning options can appear at first glance to be quite a demanding endeavor. However, as you will see later in this chapter and throughout this book, many of the estate planning techniques commonly used are relatively straightforward. We will explore some of these techniques in brief in the ensuing pages of this chapter before taking a more detailed look at these matters in later chapters.

What Does Your 'Estate' Include?

So, where do you start when it comes to making an estate plan? Well, before you decide who you want to give your assets to, you must first determine what assets you have to give away. In other words, you need to know what your estate consists of.

Simply put, your estate is comprised of everything you own—i.e. all your property and possessions, including cash, investments, insurance policies, real estate, valuables, cars, and jewelry. However, your estate also includes any liabilities that you might have, such as mortgages, car loans, outstanding utility bills and credit card bills. The total value of your estate is equal to the value of all your assets less all your liabilities.

As we will see later in this book, the total value of your estate is important when it comes to determining whether your estate will be liable to pay any estate taxes after your death.

How to Plan Your Estate

Once you have determined what assets you have in your estate, the next step will be to consider the estate planning options available to and suitable for you. Fortunately, estate planning is not as difficult or as complicated as it is often made out to be. In most cases, it simply involves a detailed analysis of your situation in life, and using that analysis to determine how you want your affairs managed if you become incapacitated and how you want your assets distributed if you die. Once you have answered these questions, you will be able to select from several devices and legal documents to put your estate plan in place.

Surprisingly, preparing the legal documents is often the easiest part of the process. The most difficult part for many people is deciding on what they want to include in their plan. This is because there are a variety of different issues to consider before finalizing your plan. At the very least, you must ask yourself (and answer) the following questions:

- What assets do I own and how much are they worth?
- How much debt do I have?
- Who should I appoint to manage my assets if I am unable to do so due to ill health?

- Who should make medical decisions on my behalf if I am unable to do so?

- Who should I appoint to take care of my minor children if I am unable to care for them myself?

- Who do I want to give my assets to when I die?

- Should I wait until I die before giving my assets away or would it be better if I did it sooner?

There are many other questions that can and should be asked. However, the questions listed above are sufficient to get you started on the road to preparing your estate plan.

Do I Need to Plan My Estate?

Many people think estate planning is only for the wealthy—believing there is no need for them to have an estate plan because they do not have many assets. But the reality is that anyone who has reached the age of majority in their state of residence, has any assets which are valuable or important to them, or who has children should make an estate plan.

In fact, there are many compelling reasons why everyone (with very few exceptions) should take the time to organize and plan their estate, regardless of whether it is large or small. For example, developing and implementing a good estate plan will ensure that:

- Your assets (including your family home, business, and investments) will be managed during any period in which you are incapacitated.

- Someone you know, and trust will be able to make medical decisions on your behalf in accordance with your specific instructions and wishes if you become incapacitated.

- Your assets will be disposed of as you would have wanted after your death.

- Your family and friends will not have to wait months or even years to receive their inheritance.

- Your children will be properly looked after by guardians of your choosing and not someone appointed by a court.

If you do not make an estate plan, a judge will make all these decisions for you. The consequences of that happening cannot be overstated. In making these decisions, the judge will look at your state's laws and the predefined estate plan that applies for everyone who fails to plan for their incapacity or the distribution of their estate. In essence, a court will appoint someone to make medical and financial decisions on your behalf if you are incapacitated, dictate who receives your assets after you die based on specific rules of inheritance (known as the rules of intestacy), appoint someone to look after your children, and much more. What is worse, neither your wishes nor those of your family can override the decisions of the court.

As you can see, one of the most compelling reasons to prepare an estate plan sooner rather than later is simply to have control. If you have a proper estate plan in place then you, and not a court, can determine how your affairs are dealt with.

We will now take a brief introductory look at some of the main issues involved in estate planning and the various estate planning devices and techniques that you may need to use to implement your plan once you have finalized your thoughts and decided on your personal strategy.

Children and Guardians

If you are a parent, your priority will probably be to arrange for the future care of your children in case you and your spouse or partner die before they grow up. You can do this by simply appointing a personal guardian who will be responsible for their care, welfare, and education. A personal guardian can be appointed under the terms of a specific guardianship agreement or under the terms of your will.

If you do not appoint a personal guardian, a court will appoint one for you. This will usually be a family member, but it may not be a family member you would have approved of to take care of your children. For this reason, it is important that you take the initiative and appoint a personal guardian of your choosing.

Apart from the day-to-day care of your children, you will also need to consider who will have day-to-day responsibility for managing any inheritances or gifts they receive, whether from you or from someone else. In many states, minor children are not allowed to own significant property or assets outright. As a result, it becomes necessary to appoint a property guardian or trustee to manage those assets on their behalf. A property guardian or trustee is different to a personal guardian in that they are only concerned with the management of the child's property and not specifically with the child's care, welfare, or education. This remains the responsibility of the personal guardian. Often, the same person is appointed as personal guardian, property guardian, and trustee. However, you may wish to separate the tasks, as many do, and assign them to those people you feel are best qualified for the job in question.

For more information on children, guardianship, and property management
options for children, please see Chapter 2.

Choosing Beneficiaries

Deciding on who will be entitled to receive your assets following your death can be an extremely rewarding and gratifying experience.

While many people simply choose to leave their estate to their spouse or children, the exact decision as to who will benefit from your estate and the manner in which your estate will pass to those beneficiaries will most likely be influenced by several factors, including whether:

- Your intended beneficiaries are minors or adults — if they are minors you should arrange to have someone manage their inheritance until they are older.

- You have any children with special needs — if so, you may wish to create a trust to provide for their long-term care.

- Your beneficiary, irrespective of his or her age, is sufficiently capable of managing a large inheritance on his or her own or whether they need assistance — again, a trust may be beneficial.

- You wish to disinherit your spouse or child — if you do, there are only a limited number of ways in which you can do this (we will look at these in later chapters).

- You want to leave something to charity — if so, you could use tax efficient trusts to leave these gifts (we discuss these in later chapters).

- There will be tax implications associated with the giving of assets to a particular beneficiary— tax can be deferred or, in some cases, avoided using specific estate planning devices.

All the above considerations, and more, will play a fundamental part in your choice as to who receives your specific assets and the way they do so. We will discuss these matters in further detail later in this book.

For more information on beneficiaries, please see Chapter 3.

Last Will and Testament

A will, more formally known as a "last will and testament," is a legal document that allows you to express your desires and intentions regarding the transfer and distribution of your real and personal property following your death. It allows you to put your wishes down "for the record" so that, should disputes or confusion arise, you may be assured that your intentions will be respected and followed after your death. In fact, both statutory and common law (laws developed by the courts rather than by statute) require that your heirs follow your documented wishes when determining how your estate is divided amongst them.

Apart from prescribing how your property should be transferred to your loved ones following your death, a will is extremely beneficial when it comes to managing property transferred to children. Under your will, you can choose from a variety of property management options for children who are to receive property. In addition, your will also affords you the opportunity to choose a personal guardian to care for your minor children after your death.

The terms of your will also usually dictate who will wind up your affairs and take charge of carrying out your instructions following your death, including your sentimental, burial, and memorial wishes. This is important as you will invariably want to ensure that the person dealing with your affairs (i.e. your executor) will honor the various choices that you have made in your will.

For those with sizeable estates, a will can play a strategic role in tax planning. The way your property is passed, how much of it is passed, and to whom it is passed determines how both the estate and the recipients of such property are taxed. A carefully drafted will can reduce estate and inheritance taxes, transfer costs, and even the general costs of probate and administration.

The primary drawback of using a will, however, is that it can take a number of months (and sometimes years) to complete the probate process—the formal process by which assets are transferred to the beneficiaries named in a will. This process often has the effect of slowing down the transfer of many of the estate's assets to the intended beneficiaries. To avoid this problem, there are numerous estate planning tools that can be utilized to avoid probate and we will discuss each of these further below.

For more information on wills, please see Chapter 4.

Executors and Probate

As briefly mentioned above, probate is the court supervised administrative process by which the assets of a deceased person are gathered, first applied towards the payment of debts, taxes and administration expenses, and then distributed to the beneficiaries named in the deceased's will. This process generally takes six to twelve months to complete, but where complexities arise it can last for years. In many cases, assets cannot or at least should not be transferred to the beneficiaries under the will until probate has been completed.

It follows, therefore, that when you make a will, you need to appoint an executor (otherwise known as a personal representative) to probate your estate following your death. Your executor will be responsible for handling, safeguarding, and distributing your property in accordance with the terms of your will. In addition, he or she will also be responsible for ensuring that any debts or taxes owed by you at the date of your death are paid by your estate. These payments, if any, are often paid from the assets of the estate before any distributions are made to the beneficiaries named in a will.

For more information on executors and probate, please see Chapter 5.

Assets that Do not Go Through Probate

If you have a spouse, child or other person that is financially dependent on you, they may need immediate access to funds from your estate if you die. As such, you will need to consider how you can transfer some or all your assets to them as quickly as possible and in a manner that avoids a potentially long probate process.

This can be achieved in several ways. Firstly, you can utilize some of the probate-free transfer devices such as pay-on-death bank accounts, transfer-on-death securities, or even life insurance policies with designated beneficiaries. In each case, you can nominate a beneficiary to receive the proceeds of the account/policy on your death. The financial institution holding those proceeds will quickly arrange the transfer of the proceeds to the named beneficiary upon production of your death certificate. These probate-free transfer methods can provide a great source of readily available funds to your family following your death.

Secondly, you could transfer your assets to a living trust. Assets held in a living trust will not become part of your probate estate because the assets are not held in your name. This allows them to be quickly distributed to the beneficiaries of the trust following your death. More on living trusts below.....

Thirdly, you can convert assets that you own solely into jointly owned assets. Where assets are jointly owned, it is possible to designate that a right of survivorship will apply to those assets. This means that when one of the joint owners die, the asset will pass directly to the surviving joint owner. The joint owner can be a friend or relative; and the assets can be comprised of anything from real estate to jewelry to cash in a bank account. Thus, in the same way as the other devices mentioned above, the surviving joint owner can quickly claim ownership of the asset following your death by simply producing a certified copy of your death certificate.

For more information on assets that do not go through probate, please see Chapter 8.

Revocable Living Trusts

A revocable living trust is a type of trust used for estate planning purposes. Under a living trust arrangement, you create a trust, declare yourself trustee of the trust, and then transfer some or all your personal property to the trust. The legal ownership of the property passes from you personally to the trust. However, as trustee of the trust you maintain control over and use of the trust property.

As creator of the living trust, you can, at any time, either revoke the trust or call for the return of some or all the property transferred to it. You can also add assets to the trust, change the terms of the trust, and even make it irrevocable (incapable of change) at any time in the future.

After your death, the trust assets will pass to the beneficiaries that you have named in the trust document in much the same way that they would under a will. Specifically, your trust document will nominate a person known as the "successor trustee" (which is a little like the executor or personal representative of an estate that passes under a will) who following your death will have the responsibility of transferring ownership of the assets in the trust to the beneficiaries named in the trust document. In most cases, the whole transfer process takes only a few weeks.

From an estate planning perspective, one of the most important features to note is that since the assets in the trust are legally owned by the trust, they will not form part of your probate estate at the time of your death. As such, there will be no need for any of these assets to go through the probate process; nor will those assets be available to settle debts from your estate (other than taxes which might be due). This, in turn, allows for the speedy distribution of those assets to the beneficiaries named in the trust document. Once all the assets are transferred to the beneficiaries, the living trust ceases to exist.

Revocable living trusts are quite easy to establish and manage, and in addition to avoiding probate there are many advantages to using living trusts as part of your overall estate plan. These reasons relate to the management of your assets during incapacity, privacy concerns, tax planning, and more.

For more information on revocable living trusts, please see Chapter 9.

Planning for Incapacity—Power of Attorney for Finance and Property

Most responsible persons plan how their property will be divided amongst their loved ones following their death. However, all these plans can go to waste if, through an accident or illness, an individual becomes incapacitated and is unable to manage his or her own affairs while still alive. For example, if you are injured in a car accident and become unconscious for a period of time, the value or some or all of your assets could become substantially depleted if they are not managed during that period. This in turn could render meaningless any plans you may have made for the distribution of your assets upon your death.

In addition, your family could be left facing serious financial hardship during your incapacity if they are unable to access family assets. For example, if your signature is required to access all or most of your family savings, then they could be without funds both to live and pay for your medical care for a significant period.

To avoid these unpleasant scenarios, you can grant a "power of attorney" to a responsible person who you trust. A power of attorney is a legal document by which you appoint and authorize another person (usually a trusted friend, family member, colleague, or adviser) to act on your behalf in the event that you become incapacitated.

For a power of attorney to apply when you are incapacitated, you must explicitly state that it is a "durable" power of attorney. While ordinary powers of attorney cease to have legal effect once you become incapacitated, a durable power of attorney remains valid—or in some cases only commences—if you become incapacitated.

Durable powers of attorney come in two forms—a durable general power of attorney and a durable limited power of attorney. Under a durable general power of attorney, you can appoint an agent to whom you give authority to: collect and disburse money on your behalf; operate your bank accounts; buy and sell property in your name; refurbish and rent out your property; and generally sign documents and deeds as your alter ego. It permits your agent to act as your authorized legal representative in relation to the whole cross-section of your legal and financial affairs, until such time as the authorization granted under the power of attorney is revoked or comes to an end.

You can limit the scope of your agent's authority by creating a durable limited power of attorney. This is like a durable general power of attorney, except that under the terms of this document you can expressly limit the agent's authority to carrying out certain functions. For example, the agent's authorized tasks could be limited to the management of your business or selling a specific piece of property such as a car or a piece of real estate at a specific price to a specific person on a specific date.

For more information on powers of attorney for finance and property, please see Chapter 6.

Planning for Incapacity—Advance Healthcare Directive

Advance healthcare directives are used to instruct others regarding the medical care that you would like to receive if you find yourself in a position where you cannot communicate your own wishes regarding the receipt of such care.

There are two specific types of healthcare directives—each with different features—that should be considered as part of your estate plan: living wills and healthcare powers of attorney.

Living Wills

A living will is a legal document by which you give healthcare providers instructions regarding the use or non-use of certain life-prolonging medical procedures in the event that you become terminally ill or permanently unconscious and are unable to communicate your wishes.

For many, the purpose of a living will is to document their wish that life-sustaining treatment—including artificially or technologically supplied nutrition and hydration—be withheld or withdrawn if they are suffering from a terminal illness, or are in a permanent state of unconsciousness from which they are unlikely to recover, and are unable to make medical decisions on their own behalf.

The way a living will works is quite straightforward. In most states, two doctors must personally examine you and agree that medical procedures will only prolong the dying process. If both doctors agree that this is the case, and if you have given instructions in your living will to do so, certain medical procedures may be withdrawn or withheld, resulting in your death. However, keep in mind that living wills can also be used to instruct attending physicians to use all possible means and treatments to keep you alive.

Other names sometimes found for living wills include "instructions," "directive to physicians," "declaration" and "advance medical directive."

Healthcare Powers of Attorney

One of the principal limitations of living wills is that they come into play only when you are either terminally ill or permanently unconscious and unable to communicate your medical wishes to your doctors. They also only deal with the receipt or non-receipt of life sustaining treatments. As such, they would not, for example, apply where you were temporarily unconscious due to a relatively minor accident.

With a healthcare power of attorney, however, you can appoint a person you know and trust to make and communicate decisions on the receipt or non-receipt of all forms of medical treatment on your behalf. You do not have to be terminally ill or permanently unconscious. You simply need to be unable to communicate your healthcare preferences. When this occurs, your appointed agent is entitled to step up and make medical decisions on your behalf.

This authority is effective only when your attending physician determines that you have lost the capacity to make informed healthcare decisions for yourself. If you still have this capacity, you retain the right to make all medical and other healthcare decisions on your behalf.

In your healthcare power of attorney, you may also limit the healthcare decisions that your agent will have authority to make. The authority of your agent to make healthcare decisions for you will generally include the authority to give informed consent, refuse to give informed consent, or to withdraw informed consent for any care, treatment, service or procedure designed to maintain, diagnose, or treat a physical or mental condition.

For more information on advanced healthcare directives, please see Chapter 7.

Reducing Taxes on Your Estate

A good estate plan will be structured in the most tax efficient manner to ensure that your estate pays as little in estate taxes as possible. Every amount paid in taxes is ultimately deducted from the amount payable from your estate to your loved ones. As such, it's very important, particularly where you have a valuable estate, that you seek tax advice when preparing your estate plan and that you utilize as many of the available tax planning opportunities as possible.

For more information on reducing taxes, please see Chapter 11.

Funeral Arrangements

Every good estate plan should encompass a funeral plan yet, despite all the obvious advantages, most people die without any form of pre-arranged plan for their funeral, burial, or cremation.

If you make your wishes known in advance, you can make sure that there is no doubt or confusion among those who are close to you as to what you would like as your final tribute. These are choices that should be only yours and it is wise to prepare them in advance.

There are several benefits to making a funeral plan. For example, you can:

- have the peace of mind of knowing that you have helped relieve your loved ones of the future worry, uncertainty, and expense of planning your funeral.
- set out your preference for burial or cremation.
- decide on your final resting place.
- make others aware of funeral and memorial arrangements that you may have already made.
- specify your wishes for the type of memorial service you would like to have.

Resource

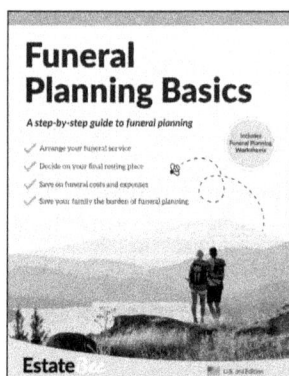

"Funeral Planning Basics - A Step-By-Step Guide to Funeral Planning"

Through proper funeral planning, you can ensure that your loved ones are not confronted with the unnecessary burden of having to plan a funeral at a time that is already very traumatic for them. This book will introduce you to issues such as organ donations, purchasing caskets, cremation, burial, purchasing grave plots, organization of funeral services, legal and financial issues, costs of prearranging a funeral, how to save money on funerals, how to finance funerals and much more.

Get your copy at:

www.estate-bee.com/product/funeral-planning-basics/

Conclusion

As you will have gathered, there are numerous benefits and satisfactions that can be derived from a good estate plan, including:

- Providing for the care and welfare of your immediate family.
- Transferring property to your beneficiaries as quickly and inexpensively as possible.
- Reducing taxes on your estate and increasing the value of the gifts made to your beneficiaries.
- Choosing the right executors and trustees for your estate.
- Minimizing stress and uncertainty for your family.
- The pleasure of benefiting a favorite charity.
- Providing for the management of inheritances received by family members/friends who need help and guidance in managing their affairs.
- Avoiding the expense and delays often associated with probate.

They say that "procrastination is the thief of time," but in estate planning procrastination is the thief of your best intentions and your assets. If you procrastinate for too long and put off planning your estate, it becomes very unlikely that your property will be distributed entirely as you would have wished, and becomes very likely that your family and friends will suffer personally and financially. So, do not procrastinate—take some simple steps to begin the process of creating your estate plan today. In the following chapters, we will provide more detail about the estate planning options you have to select from.

CHAPTER 2

Children, Guardians and Property Management

What Is a Guardian?

A guardian is the person responsible for a child's (or other dependent or incapacitated person's) physical care, education, health, and welfare; as well as for making decisions about the child's faith-related matters. In some states, a non-parent guardian is called a "conservator."

Normally, if you are married and have a child, you and your spouse are the primary legal guardians of your minor children—including any children that you may have adopted together. If you die, then your surviving spouse becomes the sole guardian of these children. However, should your surviving spouse also die and neither of you have made any provisions for the appointment of a guardian, then the children could become the responsibility of the court. Where this happens, there is a real risk that your children will end up being cared for by people that you would never have wished to raise them.

If you have children, it is vital to plan and ensure that they will be properly cared for if neither you nor your spouse are around to do so. In this respect, you should give careful thought and consideration to naming a guardian and an alternate guardian in your will to take care of your children following your death.

Sole and Joint-Guardians

You have the option of appointing one or more guardians to care for your children. If you appoint one guardian, he or she will be known as a "sole guardian" and will be solely responsible for the welfare of your children and for making all decisions on their behalf. Alternatively, you can nominate two or more people to serve as joint guardians to your children. However, for joint guardians to legally make decisions regarding children in their care, each of them must agree on the decision to be made. This may be easier said than done. For this reason, joint guardians are usually only nominated where they are married to each other or live together, as well as where they each have an important relationship to the children (uncles or aunts, for example).

If you are considering appointing a married couple as joint-guardians of your children, be sure to carefully consider the status of the couple's relationship and whether you would want both spouses to serve as guardians if they ever separated or divorced. In such instances, it may be preferable to simply appoint one spouse as guardian at the very outset. The choice, however, is yours.

Alternate Guardians

When appointing a guardian, it is generally recommended that you also appoint an alternate guardian (or several alternates, hierarchically) who will serve if your first named guardian (known as your "primary guardian") is unable or unwilling to serve for any reason when the time comes. If your first choice guardian cannot serve and you fail to name an alternate guardian in your will, it will then fall to the court to step in and determine who will act as guardian to your children. As mentioned above, the court's appointee may not be someone that you would have approved of had you the opportunity to do so.

As with your choice of primary guardians, you may also nominate an alternate guardian to serve alone or may name two or more to serve jointly with each other. Remember, your choice of alternate guardian is every bit as important as your choice of primary guardian.

Appointment of a Guardian

In most cases, a guardian can be appointed under the terms of your will by simply adding a standard guardianship clause. This will go some way towards ensuring that your children are cared for by someone who shares your values and ideals and who will properly care for your children. However, simply nominating a person to act as a guardian under your will is by no means absolute. It does not guarantee that your nominee will automatically become the legal guardian of your children. The final decision as to whether your nominee will be permitted to become the legal guardian of your children rests with a judge in the state where your children reside. For this very reason, it is often recommended that you explain (in a letter of intent or wishes) the rationale for nominating a particular person to act as guardian, stating specifically why you believe the nominee would be most suitable for the role. These types of explanations can have a significant impact on the court's approval of your nominee.

Did You Know

As well as being able to appoint guardians under your will, it is also possible to appoint guardians by means of a written guardianship agreement made between the parent(s) of a child and the proposed guardian(s).

You may also nominate different guardians to look after different interests of your children, e.g. financial, educational, spiritual, etc. In this way, you can choose to give your children the best part of each of your guardians.

Who Can Be a Guardian?

The short answer is that anyone can be a guardian, if they are an adult who is agreeable to acting as a guardian to your children. However, the fact that someone is eligible to be appointed as a guardian does not of itself mean that a court would accept that person's nomination as a guardian. For example, a court would be unlikely to accept the nomination of a person with a history of child abuse or serious criminal activity.

Should You Appoint a Guardian for Your Minor Children?

Absolutely. If you have children under the age of majority in your state, then you should appoint a responsible guardian to take care of them should it be necessary. Absent doing so, a court will make its own appointment for you.

The age of majority for each state is set out in the table below.

Age of Majority in the United States	
Age 18	Alaska, Arizona, California, Colorado, Connecticut, District of Columbia, Florida, Georgia, Hawaii, Idaho, Illinois, Indiana, Iowa, Kansas, Kentucky, Louisiana, Maine, Maryland, Massachusetts, Michigan, Minnesota, Missouri, Montana, New Hampshire, New Mexico, New Jersey, New York, North Carolina, North Dakota, Oklahoma, Oregon, Pennsylvania, Rhode Island, South Carolina, South Dakota, Texas, Vermont, Washington, West Virginia and Wyoming.
Age 19	Alabama, Delaware, and Nebraska.
Age 21	Mississippi.
Graduation or 18 (whichever occurs first)	Ohio and Utah.
Graduation or 18 (whichever occurs later)	Arkansas, Tennessee, and Virginia.
Graduation or 18 (whichever occurs first) or 19 if still at school	Nevada and Wisconsin.

What to Consider When Choosing a Guardian for Your Child

As you will be leaving the responsibility of caring for your children to another person, the decision as to whom you appoint as a guardian is an extremely important one; and one that should not be made lightly. While you need to take many factors into consideration, you should ultimately choose the person you believe will offer the best care and support to your children. Often this will be a close relative or family friend. However, before appointing them as guardian under your will, it is important that you check with your proposed nominee to ensure that he or she is willing to accept such a responsible and onerous role. There is no point in nominating someone if you think they will refuse to accept the role when the time comes.

Important Tip

Discuss your choice of guardian with your proposed guardian(s) before nominating them in your will, and make sure each of them is genuinely willing to accept the responsibility should it become necessary.

There are many factors to consider in deciding whether a person would be the right person to appoint as a guardian to your children. You should ask yourself the following questions regarding your proposed nominee:

- Is the person you are considering willing to accept the long-term responsibility of being a guardian to your children? If the person is not willing or is not fully committed, you need to consider someone else.

- Is this person responsible and up to the task of raising your children?

- Is the person an adult? A minor cannot act as a legal guardian for another minor.

- Where does this person live?

- Would your children be uprooted and moved away from their friends and family members if they went to live with this guardian? Would that be in their best interests?

- If you have more than one child, do you want your children to remain together? If you do, then be sure to name the same guardian for all your children. Bear in mind that judges are often wary of separating siblings and they do have the ultimate say in the matter.

- What is this person's home situation? For example, does he or she have a house or a one-bed apartment? Is the potential guardian in a stable relationship?

- Will the potential guardian be able to provide your children with a stable positive environment and home life?

- Will your children still have easy access to their other relatives—such as grandparents?

- What is the person's religious and moral beliefs?

- Does the person have any medical conditions or other issues that would prevent them from being a suitable guardian?

- If you cannot make sufficient provision for your children's long-term care, will this person be able to afford to care for your children?

These are all important and relevant questions, but only the tip of the iceberg regarding the investigation you should make and issues you should consider before selecting someone as your children's guardian.

Once you have selected someone to act as a guardian to your children, it is important to discuss the potential appointment with him or her (or them) in detail. While most people are flattered, you will find that some are unable or unwilling to accept the responsibility. Be wary also of people agreeing to accept the role insincerely in the expectation that they will never be called upon to act. This is another particularly good reason to appoint an alternate guardian—just in case the primary guardian is unable or unwilling to assume the role when the time comes.

Again, we must stress that naming a person as guardian in a will is merely a nomination, not the actual appointment (even though the word "appoint" will often be used in the guardian clause of a will). A court will still need to approve the appointment of the guardian you nominated. In the normal course, the court will usually ratify the appointment of a person nominated in a will. However, it is always possible that interested family members or other parties may challenge the appointment. Were this to happen, the court would listen to all relevant parties before making a determination as to whether the nomination should stand or whether it would be in the best interests of the children to have another person appointed as guardian. Usually, the court will appoint the person nominated in the will unless it finds compelling reasons not to do so. The court is concerned primarily with the best interests of the children.

Given the requirement for court approval and the potential of challenge, it is important that you specify, either in your will or on a separate document, the reasons for appointing the guardian in question. This will have a strong persuasive effect when being considered by the court.

If you are not married to the other parent of your minor child, it is important to understand that the nomination of a guardian in your will does not of itself grant priority to your guardian over the rights of the surviving parent if you die. In most cases, the surviving parent's rights will take priority over the rights of your nominated guardian.

What Happens if No Guardian Is Named in Your Will?

If you do not name a guardian for your children under the terms of your will, or elsewhere in a legal document, then the courts will decide who is best placed to act as their guardian. The courts usually give preference to family members based on the family member's relationship to the children. In most cases, if available and willing, the children's other parent is the automatic first choice to care for them. However, if the other parent is unwilling or unable to act, the courts will look at other family members.

In circumstances where you are separated or divorced, or where you are essentially a single parent, you may not want your child's other parent to have custody or guardianship rights over your child. This may be because you feel that the other parent is incapable or will not properly care for your child. You may feel that the other parent has effectively abandoned your child which therefore makes them an illogical choice for guardian. If you anticipate that such a situation may arise, contact an attorney or legal aid service as they will be able to advise you appropriately and may even draft a pre-emptive guardianship agreement for your child that, hopefully, the court will later approve. You will also want to document your reasons for wishing the other parent to remain out of the picture. At times, a court will grant custody to someone other than a surviving parent if it is satisfied that the surviving parent has legally abandoned the child (by not providing for or visiting that child for an extended period of time) or that the surviving parent is unfit or unsuitable to properly care for the child.

Where the other parent is not available or deemed to be unsuitable, the court will look next to the child's grandparents, aunts or uncles, adult siblings, or other relatives to see if they would be a suitable guardian. Remember, however, that a court will not know your children or your wishes for them. As such, if you believe that any of these relatives would be unsuitable (for whatever reason) you should visit your attorney with a view to making legal arrangements for someone else to care for your child.

Important Tip

If you are concerned that a relative might legally challenge your decision about your choice of guardian for your children, we recommend that you contact a suitably qualified attorney to discuss your situation.

Management of Children's Property

While the appointment of a guardian to care for and to raise your child is important, it is equally important to consider who will manage the money and property your child inherits from you; and indeed from anyone else. As mentioned earlier, children who have not yet reached the age of majority lack sufficient legal capacity to receive and manage inherited property. While this lack of capacity is often not an issue for most minors, it is problematic where they inherit significant or valuable assets. In such cases, it will be necessary to appoint an adult called a "custodian," "trustee," or "property guardian" to receive and manage the property on behalf of the minor.

If you don't make arrangements to provide for the future management of your children's property, the court will do it for you by appointing a "property guardian" of its choosing to manage the inheritances they receive. Like the situation with personal guardians, a court will often appoint the surviving parent, but this is not always the case. A third party or court appointed guardian can be appointed to deal with the property and, in such cases, that property guardian will have complete control over your children's inheritance. As such, it is important that you deal with this appointment in your will or in another legal agreement.

Options for Property Management

Fortunately, it is relatively easy and straightforward to avoid the uncertainties and hassles of a court-appointed guardianship. You can choose someone now to manage any property that your minor or young adult children may someday inherit from you. While there are many ways that you can structure this arrangement, four of the simplest and most used methods are listed below.

Appointment of a Property Guardian

A property guardian is a person you appoint to be responsible for managing the property you leave to your children plus any other property that your children might receive. A property guardian is obligated to manage the property in your children's best interests, using it to pay for their normal living expenses, as well as their health and educational needs.

If you name a property guardian for your children in your will, when the time comes the court will (in the absence of strong reasons to do otherwise) formally appoint your selected person as property guardian to your children.

While a property guardian is appointed under the terms of your will, the scope of his or her management authority extends beyond the management of property left to your children under your will. In fact, it extends to include any property later received by your children where there are no pre-existing arrangements for management of that property (such as under a trust). As such, should your children receive an inheritance from a long lost relative, their property guardian is authorized to manage that property in the absence of your relative having provided for a specific means of management.

Remember, a property guardian is not the same as a personal guardian, who is responsible for the care, health, welfare, and education of a child. A property guardian is only responsible for managing a child's property—although he or she can apply the managed property for the benefit of the child's care, health, welfare, or education. Do not make the mistake of appointing only a property guardian and thinking that he or she will also be responsible for the day-to-day care of the child.

Uniform Transfer to Minors' Act

As often mentioned, minors in most states do not have the legal capacity to enter into certain legal contracts, and are therefore not in a position where they can own and manage assets such as stocks, bonds, funds, life insurance receipts and other annuities. It is therefore important to recognize that you cannot simply transfer any of these types of items directly to your minor children; or indeed to any other minor.

One of the most common methods used to get around this problem comes in the form of a custodianship created under either the Uniform Gift to Minors Act ("UGMA") or the Uniform Transfer to Minors Act ("UTMA"). Rather than transferring assets directly to your children on your death, you transfer your assets to a custodian who will hold those assets in trust for your children until they reach a pre-determined age. Once your children reach this age, the custodian will transfer the property that he or she is holding on their behalf to them. In the interim period, the custodian will be obliged to manage the property on your children's behalf in accordance with the provisions set out in the UGMA/UTMA.

The UGMA, which was enacted before the UTMA, created a simple way for assets to be transferred to children under a trust arrangement without the need for lawyers and without the associated legal costs. To set up a custodianship under the UGMA, all a person needed to do was identify the property which he or she wished to transfer to a child (it can be any child named under a will or trust—not just the child of the testator or grantor) and to name a custodian to manage that property in the event that the child in question had not reached a designated age (usually between 18 to 25 years depending on state law) at the time they became entitled to receive the gift.

A typical clause of this type would be as follows:

"I give $25,000 to James Jones, as custodian for Sarah Parker under the California Uniform Transfers to Minors Act, to hold until Sarah Parker reaches the age of 21 years."

While the UTMA is similar in its approach to the UGMA, it is widely considered to be more flexible than the UGMA, which was repealed to a large degree by the UTMA. While the UTMA affords minors much of the same benefits as the previous act, it also allows minors to own other types of property (apart from cash) such as real estate, patents and royalties, and more importantly for the transfers to occur through inheritance and not simply by means of a gift.

The UTMA has been adopted in all states except for South Carolina.

The age at which the custodianship terminates is the age at which a minor becomes legally entitled to call for the assets held by a custodian to be transferred to him or her, and to have the custodial trust terminated. The table below shows the ages of termination of custodianships in the various states which have adopted the UTMA. As you will see, the ages vary from 18 to 25 years of age. You will also see that in some states the age is specified, while in other states a range of ages is provided from which the will or trust maker can chose a particular age.

You should be aware that the age of termination of a custodianship is not necessarily the same as the age of majority in a particular state.

Age Limits for Property Management in UTMA States			
State	**Age of Receipt**	**State**	**Age of Receipt**
Alabama	21	Montana	21
Alaska	18 to 25	Nebraska	21
Arizona	21	Nevada	18 to 25
Arkansas	18 to 21	New Hampshire	21
California	18 to 25	New Jersey	18 to 21
Colorado	21	New Mexico	21
Connecticut	21	New York	21
Delaware	21	North Carolina	18 to 21

District of Columbia	18 to 21	North Dakota	21
Florida	21	Ohio	18 to 21
Georgia	21	Oklahoma	18 to 21
Hawaii	21	Oregon	21 to 25
Idaho	21	Pennsylvania	21 to 25
Illinois	21	Rhode Island	21
Indiana	21	South Dakota	18
Iowa	21	Tennessee	21 to 25
Kansas	21	Texas	21
Kentucky	18	Utah	21
Maine	18 to 21	Vermont	18 to 21
Maryland	21	Virginia	18 to 21, or 25
Massachusetts	21	Washington	21 or 25
Michigan	18 to 21	West Virginia	21
Minnesota	21	Wisconsin	21
Mississippi	**21**	Wyoming	**21 to 30**
Missouri	21		

Individual Child Trusts

A child's trust is valid in all states and can be created under the terms of a will (such trusts are often called a "testamentary trust") or a living trust (which are known as "child sub-trusts").

A trust is a fiduciary arrangement whereby a person is appointed to become the legal owner of trust property, which they will hold for the benefit of another person. A child trust is a trust created for the benefit of a child. You can create a separate child trust for each of your children (if you wish) and for any other minor who stands to inherit under the terms of your will or living trust.

In your will or living trust document, you can name a trustee (usually a trusted relative or friend) who will manage the inheritance that a child will receive (as a beneficiary of that trust) until that child reaches an age specified by you. If the child in question has reached that age at the time of your death, and is past the age of majority for their state, the trust never actually comes into existence and the property is instead transferred directly to them upon your death.

However, where your child is under the age specified in your will or trust document, the inheritance will be transferred to a separate trust fund and will be managed by the nominated trustee in accordance with provisions set out in your will or trust document. The trustee will continue to manage the trust property until the child in question has reached the age specified in your will or trust document. At that time, the remainder of the trust property will be transferred to the now adult beneficiary and the trust will be terminated.

During the trust, the trustee will have broad discretion over the management and distribution of the trust property. If the trustee deems it appropriate, he or she can release monies to or make payments on behalf of the child to cover matters ranging from education, medical and general maintenance.

While court supervision is generally not required with these types of trusts, serving as a trustee can be more onerous than simply serving as a custodian under the UTMA. For example, a trustee is required to file annual income tax returns for the child trust with the IRS. Also, because the powers of trustees of a child's trust are set out in the will or trust document itself, it will be necessary for the trustee to produce copies of the relevant document every time he or she has to deal with a financial institution on behalf of the minor child. By contrast, given that the powers of a UTMA custodian are provided for under statute, most banks and other institutions are more familiar with their terms and are more knowledgeable of the authority given to custodians under these statutes.

Children's Pot Trusts

A pot trust is a good tool to use with younger children. Pot trusts are a legal device that allows you to place monies in trust to benefit two or more of your minor children. Pot trusts, however, are somewhat unique in that trust assets are made available to whichever child needs them most rather than being divided equally for the benefit of each child. With a pot trust, your trustee has discretion to apportion the trust funds between the children as he or she sees fit. So, for example, if one of your children wishes to go to college, your trustee can take a portion of the money from the trust to send that child to college. Similarly, should one of your children require an expensive medical treatment, monies can be released from the trust to cover the costs of the treatment.

A pot trust will terminate when the youngest child reaches a specified age (known as the age of termination of the trust), usually 18 to 30 years of age. At that time, the trust is divided between the children equally.

One of the principal drawbacks to using a pot trust is that older children will not receive their share of the balance of the trust property until the youngest child reaches the designated age of termination of the trust. As such, they may well be into adulthood by the time they receive their shares of the inheritance.

Providing for Children with Special Needs

Millions of families in the United States have special needs children. These children, who often require care well after they reach the age of majority and sometimes for their entire lives, present a unique estate planning challenge that if not met could have disastrous financial results. Yet many parents of special needs children do not prepare a proper estate plan designed to meet those unique circumstances. Given the daily difficulties faced by these parents, this is understandable, but even more difficulties may arise from the failure to plan.

The most important thing that parents of special needs children need to understand is the strict conditions mandated by federal statutes for a special needs person to be eligible for federal government benefits, as well as the ways in which the failure to create a proper estate plan could result in the failure to meet those conditions and the subsequent loss of those important benefits (which in many cases can cover a large portion of the expenses incurred in caring for a special needs child).

For example, one of the key conditions for federal government benefits and services—such as Medicaid and Supplemental Security Income (SSI)—is that a special needs child cannot have more than a set amount of assets in his or her own name. In 2025, this amount is only $2,000 in the case of SSI, while the eligibility limit for Medicaid varies state by state and can be as low as $2,000. Therefore, if your special needs child receives a gift or inheritance worth more than $2,000, the child could lose most, if not all, of his or her government benefits.

If you are the parent of a child with special needs, you can circumvent this adverse result by creating a "special needs trust" as part of your estate plan. The purpose of this trust is to provide for the child (or adult) without risking that person's eligibility for federal benefits—including the valuable and important healthcare coverage.

Special Needs Trust

With a special needs trust, the trustee will hold legal title to the assets for the benefit of the person with special needs, who is the beneficiary. As such, when it comes to assessing the person's entitlement to federal benefits, these assets will not be taken into consideration. Meanwhile, the trustee will be authorized under the terms of the special needs trust document to spend the funds held in trust on behalf of and generally to provide for the person with special needs.

Keep in mind that Medicaid and SSI officials review trust expenditures to determine whether they are appropriate. The funds in a special needs trust can be used to pay for anything from medical expenses not covered by SSI and Medicaid to vacations and entertainment if the expenditure benefits the named beneficiary.

One way to fund the special needs trust is with a life insurance policy and/or an employee retirement plan designating the trust as beneficiary. This, along with the trust itself, has the added benefit of avoiding probate with respect to the life insurance proceeds and other trust assets when you die.

Bear in mind that relatives such as grandparents must also take care to leave gifts or inheritances to the special needs trust rather than your child to preserve eligibility for government programs.

In addition, a trust can give you the peace of mind of knowing that a caring and qualified individual will be acting as trustee and watching over your child's money. As such, when choosing a trustee for a special needs trust, it is important that you select a person who is familiar with the special needs of your child (including the various medical requirements and medical and social services personnel, benefits and services involved). At the same time, you want someone who can handle the financial and legal requirements of the position. Therefore, many special needs families name co-trustees, one of whom knows the child personally and one of whom has the financial wherewithal required. In any event, given the long period of time the trust may be operational, it is important to name an alternate trustee in case the initial trustee becomes unable or unwilling to perform the duties of the job.

It should be emphasized that the rules governing special needs trusts are complicated and vary by state. In addition, planning in this area requires an in-depth knowledge of both the law and the range of federal benefits available to special needs children. Therefore, while you can theoretically do the research and prepare the trust document yourself, we recommend that you consult with a special needs legal specialist to assist you. Fortunately, there are now legal and financial professionals who specialize in guiding families through the intricate maze of federal and state programs for disabled individuals, and who also help set up trusts, obtain insurance policies, and prepare other estate planning documents.

Letter of Guidance

In addition to the special needs trust it is a good idea to create a "letter of guidance" (sometimes called a "letter of intent"), which provides information and instructions to your child's guardian, trustee, and caregivers. This letter is neither a legal requirement nor a legal document, but it provides everything these individuals should know about your child's special needs, including medical diagnosis, treatment and medications, specific likes, and dislikes, etc.

You should also create a computer file and/or binder containing all the documents and information about your child's condition, medical history, doctors and other caregivers, government benefits and agencies, etc. that will be necessary or helpful for those caring for your child in the future.

Appointment as Guardian of Adult Special Needs Child

When your special needs child turns 18 years of age, you should also create a power-of-attorney and/or guardianship documents with respect to your child's finances and healthcare, naming yourself as your child's agent or guardian. Without these documents in place, when your child turns 18 you may not be able to have access to his or her medical records or make healthcare and financial decisions. Government and other benefits may also change in the case of an adult child, so you should familiarize yourself with the applicable rules and regulations.

Choosing a Trustee

A trustee's duties can continue for a number of years and, in many cases, may require expertise in investing money, dealing with real estate, paying bills, filing accounts, and managing money on behalf of the trusts underlying beneficiaries. As such, you will need to carefully consider your choice of proposed trustee. In many cases, people who establish a trust choose a family member or close friend as they tend not to charge fees for carrying out the role. This is fine so long as the person can handle the financial matters involved and has sufficient time to carry out the role—and of course is willing to do so...remember to check with them first.

Professional trustees, on the other hand, will charge annual management fees for providing trustee services. In some instances, these fees can be quite substantial. However, given the expertise that a professional trustee can bring to the table, it is important to at least consider engaging them where you have a large estate.

If you decide not to engage a professional trustee and opt for a family member or friend instead, then the characteristics that you should look for in your nominee are honesty, intelligence, diligence, and conscientiousness. Having these qualities, above all else, will at least go some way towards ensuring that you pick the right person for the job.

Trustee's Duties

Trustees have many duties attached to their role. A trustee occupies a fiduciary position (a position of trust) and is therefore bound to act for the benefit of another. Some specific duties include the following:

Duty to Adhere to the Terms of the Trust

While this may appear to be an obvious statement, it is surprising how often trustees' decisions are made without referring to the documents establishing the trust. The trust documents should indicate whether the act in question is permitted under the terms of the trust or not.

Duty to Act Personally

Unless the trust terms permit, trustees must act personally and may not delegate the performance of tasks or the making of decisions concerning the trust—although the trustee is normally permitted to take professional advice where required.

Duty to Act in the Best Interests of the Beneficiaries

A trustee is required to act impartially and in the best interests of the trust's beneficiaries. If a trustee fails to do so, he or she could find themselves exposed to a lawsuit instituted by a beneficiary seeking a court review of the trustee's acts and/or omissions. Such a review could result in the trustee losing any compensation which he or she was entitled to receive under the terms of the trust document or even in the trustee being removed from office.

Duty to Account

Trustees are required to keep full and proper records of the trust—including all transactions carried out by the trust and all distributions and returns made by it.

Duty to Supply Information

The beneficiaries of a trust are entitled to certain information regarding the trust. While you may, in your will or living trust document, specify the precise information to which your beneficiaries are entitled, they are usually entitled to a copy of the trust deed, latest financial accounts, copies of title documents relating to trust assets, and details of distributions made from the trust to beneficiaries. However, trustees are not normally required to provide explanations for their decisions, minutes of trustee meetings (if any), correspondence between trustees and other beneficiaries, or a copy of any memorandum of wishes provided by the creator of the trust.

Duty to Invest Prudently

In managing the affairs of others, trustees are required to exercise the due care, diligence, and skill that a prudent person would ordinarily exercise in the management of other people's assets. This applies equally in the context of investing the trust's assets.

As a trustee is under a duty to preserve the value of the trust's assets, he or she may need to make appropriate investments to avoid deflation and devaluation of the trust assets. The trustee must exercise due care and diligence in choosing the investments; and where appropriate should obtain professional investment advice.

Duty to Carry Out Duties Without Payment

Save in respect of out of pocket expenses, trustees are generally required to act without payment unless the trust terms provide otherwise. This is partly why so many people appoint friends and relatives as trustees. Professional trustees, on other hand, will always ensure that the trust documentation contains appropriate powers for the trustee to receive remuneration before they act.

Duty to Not Benefit Personally from the Trust

As a fiduciary, a trustee may not benefit personally unless the trust document specifically allows for this. This is echoed by the requirement that trustees act in good faith and avoid conflicts of interest which could adversely affect the trustee's decisions. If a conflict of interest does arise, the trustee should always act carefully and should consider taking professional advice. In certain instances, the trustee may be able to act where he has made a full disclosure of his interests to all beneficiaries and has obtained their written consent to the transaction in question which gives rise to the conflict.

CHAPTER 3

Gifts and Beneficiaries

Gifting Your Assets

Once you have taken the time to make a list of all your assets, the next step in the estate planning process is to consider who you want to gift those assets to. For the most part, you are free to gift your assets as you wish. However, there are some restrictions on this freedom. For example, in many states, spouses have a legal entitlement to a certain proportion of their deceased spouse's estate. So, if you are married, this is something that you will need to consider when preparing your distribution plan.

Further issues arise in the context of children. Under the laws of many states, if you fail to make provision for your children, they may be able to successfully litigate against your estate and obtain an order providing for the redistribution of your assets to include an appropriate share for them. There are ways to get around this risk, and we will look at them later in this chapter.

Another thing that you will need to keep in mind when making gifts is the age of the beneficiary. As mentioned earlier, most states impose restrictions on minor beneficiaries receiving substantial assets. As such, it becomes necessary to appoint a trustee or guardian who will manage the minor's inheritance until he or she becomes old enough to do so.

As you will have gathered, there are rules and legalities surrounding the making of gifts. So, to properly prepare your estate plan, you need to have at least a broad understanding of how a gift can be made and what matters might impact the making of that gift. We will look at these issues in the ensuing pages.

How to Make a Gift

There are three principal ways in which you can make a gift to someone following your death: under a will; under a living trust; or under a survivorship designation (e.g. life insurance policies, pay-on-death accounts, joint tenancies, etc.). While a survivorship designation is relatively straightforward, the making of gifts under both wills and living trusts is a little more complicated and there are some basic 'gifting rules' which need to be followed. You will also need to have a general understanding of the types of gifts that can be made under a will and living trust, as well as the different types of beneficiaries under each device. We will examine each of these in turn below.

Types of Gifts

A gift can generally be defined as a voluntary transfer of property from one person to another made gratuitously, without any consideration or compensation. Under your will or living trust, you can leave gifts of either financial or personal value to your family and friends. These gifts can come in the form of gifts of a specific item, gifts of cash, or gifts of the residuary of your estate or trust estate.

Important Note

Your estate is the total sum of your possessions, property and money held in your name, minus the total sum of your personal debts, at the time of your death. Your trust estate, on the other hand, means all the assets owned by a trust (such as your living trust) at the time of your death.

The main classifications of gifts are set out below.

Specific Item Gifts

A specific item gift (also known as a demonstrative legacy or specific bequest) is a gift of a specific item to a named beneficiary. Gifts of this type typically include specific items of personal property you own such as a car, a piece of jewelry, stocks, bonds, real estate and so on. When drafting your will or living trust, it is important to ensure that you clearly identify and describe the property that you wish to gift. For example, if you are gifting a car, you should describe the make, model, and color of the car rather than simply referring to "my car." This reduces the risk of confusion over what you intended—especially if you have more than one car at the time of your death. When writing a provision for a gift, a good question to ask yourself is whether a stranger reading your will or living trust would easily understand exactly what you wanted to gift. If not, you need to re-write that clause.

Cash Gifts

A cash gift (also known as a monetary or pecuniary legacy) is a gift of a specific amount of money or cash to a named beneficiary. Just as with specific items gifts, when making a cash gift you need to clearly specify the amount that you are gifting (including the currency) and the person to whom you wish to make the gift to. In addition, when making a cash gift, it is important that you consider the financial implications on the overall estate. Specifically, you need to ensure that sufficient funds are readily available to meet the needs of your dependents or to discharge any taxes or expenses (including funeral expenses) which might be payable following your death. So be careful not to exhaust your cash too quickly—otherwise, other assets may need to be sold to raise funds to discharge these obligations.

Gift of the Residuary Estate

This is simply a gift of the residue of an estate or trust estate to one or more named beneficiaries. The residue of an estate (or residuary estate, as it is often called) is the remainder of a deceased person's estate after the payment of all debts, funeral and testamentary expenses, and after all specific item and cash gifts have been made. The residue of your trust estate is the same except that it is the balance of your trust estate after all specific gifts and payments have been made from your trust.

Important Note

The residue of an estate or trust estate is that part of the estate or trust estate which remains after the payment of all debts and expenses, and after making the transfer of all specific gifts and cash gifts.

A residuary also includes property that is the subject of a failed gift. A gift fails in circumstances where the beneficiary has died (and no alternate beneficiary is named) or refuses their right to the gift. The person entitled to receive a gift of the residuary estate under a will or residuary trust estate under a living trust is called the residuary beneficiary or, if there is more than one beneficiary, residuary beneficiaries.

Types of Beneficiaries

A beneficiary is a person, organization or other entity that will inherit part of your assets or estate under your will or living trust.

There are three principal types of beneficiaries under a will or living trust: a specific gift beneficiary, an alternate beneficiary, and a residuary beneficiary.

Specific Gift Beneficiary

A specific gift beneficiary is a person or organization named in your will or living trust to receive a specific item gift or a specific cash gift as defined above. Specific gifts are generally the first gifts distributed under a will or living trust. Any assets that are not specifically distributed under your will or living trust form part of the residue (assuming that you have a catch-all residuary clause—see below) and will usually be given (unless there are taxes or other expenses to be discharged) to the person or persons named as residuary beneficiaries in each case.

Alternate Beneficiary

When naming beneficiaries to receive gifts under your will or living trust, it's prudent (but not obligatory) to prepare for the possibility that one or more of these beneficiaries will be unable (whether due to death or otherwise) or unwilling (for whatever reason) to accept the gifts made to them. To this end, it is helpful to nominate alternate beneficiaries to receive the gift if the primary beneficiary is unable or unwilling to do so. An alternate beneficiary is a person who becomes legally entitled to inherit a gift if the first named beneficiary is unable or unwilling to accept the gift. Alternate beneficiaries are the second class of beneficiaries to inherit under your will or living trust.

A beneficiary who refuses to accept a gift is said to have "disclaimed" their entitlement to a gift. It is advisable to have all such disclaimers in writing before the gift is passed to the alternate beneficiary.

Here are a few examples of situations where it might make sense to name alternate beneficiaries:

- You have left something to someone who has a dangerous occupation and there is a risk that this person might predecease you.

- You have left something substantial or meaningful to somebody older than you who is likely to predecease you.

- You have left a gift to someone with an illness that may or may not claim their lives.

You are entirely free to name more than one person as an alternate beneficiary. You can even appoint a second alternate to receive a gift where the first alternate is unable or unwilling to accept it. However, when doing this it is important that you fully consider the order in which the alternate beneficiaries become entitled to share the property and ensure that this order is correct.

Residuary Beneficiary

A residuary beneficiary is the person(s) or organization(s) named to receive the residue of your estate or trust estate. The residuary beneficiaries get what is left when all the specific gifts and cash gifts have been made and all debts, expenses and taxes have been paid.

Who May Not Be a Beneficiary?

While you are generally free to make gifts to anyone you choose, the law does place some restrictions on the people who can receive gifts from you under your will. In particular, the following persons or organizations will be precluded from receiving gifts under your will:

- A lawyer who is involved in drafting your will or in providing counsel to you in connection with it.

- Any person who acts as a witness to the signing of your will, as well as the spouses of such witnesses.

- Any person who unlawfully caused your death.

- An unincorporated association that is not permitted to hold property.

If a lawyer is permitted to receive a gift under the terms of your will, the presumption will be raised, as a matter of law, that your lawyer exerted some form of undue influence over you which caused you to name him or her as a beneficiary under your will. To prevent such abuses of influence, lawyers involved in the preparation of a will are prohibited from inheriting under it. Therefore, if you have a lawyer relative or friend that you wish to benefit under your will, it is advisable that you hire a third-party attorney to draft your will for you; and that you simply don't consult with or engage your lawyer relative or friend in relation to the matter. It's important to note, however, that this prohibition on making gifts to your lawyer friend or relative does not prevent you appointing them as your executor or directing that they be paid for carrying out their duties as executor.

The prohibition against witnesses (and their spouses) inheriting under your will has its origins in old English rules of evidence, upon which U.S. common law is partly based. These rules stipulated that parties nominated as beneficiaries under a will could not testify in court as to its proper execution due to their conflict of interest. This is because there was a fear that their testimony could be influenced by the value of the gifts that the testator left to them under the will. If they stood to inherit a windfall, the witnesses were considered more likely to testify that all the formalities associated with signing the will were strictly complied with and that, as a result, the will was valid. Of course, the opposite scenario is also possible.

As a result of these rules, gifts to witnesses or their spouses under a will are rendered null and void in most states. It is therefore recommended that none of the witnesses to your will, their spouses, or even their relatives, should stand to benefit under your will as they will most likely be prohibited from receiving the gift made to them. If you wish to leave them a gift, it's recommended that you either use alternative witnesses or that you leave the gift to them under the terms of a codicil and that other people witness your execution of that codicil.

Did You Know

A codicil is a document that amends, rather than replaces, a previously executed will. The formalities associated with executing a codicil are almost identical to that associated with executing a will.

The prohibition against making gifts to an unincorporated association that is not permitted to hold property is important to note in the context of making gifts to clubs and other unincorporated organizations. Before you make gifts to such organizations, you should check with the secretary of that organization to ensure it has sufficient powers to receive the gift.

Changing Beneficiaries

One of the main advantages of having a will or a revocable living trust is that you can change the terms of each document at any time you want provided you are mentally competent to do so. In fact, subject to complying with any applicable state laws which require you to leave a specific portion of your estate to your spouse and children, you are completely free to chop and change the beneficiaries named in your documents and the gifts made to them as often as you like.

While most people do not chop and change beneficiaries and gifts regularly, there will be circumstances where changes are required. For example, you may wish to amend your will or living trust if: -

- one or more of your named beneficiaries die before you.

- an executor, trustee, guardian, or custodian named in your will dies before you.

- you dispose of a specific item of property that you had earmarked under your will for a particular beneficiary.

- you wish to add new beneficiaries or change existing ones.

- you wish to make new gifts.

Amending your will and trust documents is a relatively straightforward exercise. To amend your will, you can either make a new will in its entirety (which automatically revokes your old will) or you can make a codicil which will amend a specific portion of your existing will. The codicil itself simply sets out the specific changes that are being made to your will. The codicil will need to be executed in compliance with the same formalities that applied to the execution of your will.

Living trusts, on the other hand, can be amended by an amendment agreement (if the trust was created under an agreement) or a deed of amendment (if the trust was created under a deed). Again, like a codicil, the agreement or deed simply records details of the specific changes that are being made to the original trust document.

Gifts to Spouses

Before making a gift to your spouse, or indeed to anyone, it is important to understand the rights which surviving spouses have over their deceased spouse's estate, as well as the basic differences in distribution of property in both common law and community property states. We will look at these matters below.

Community Property States

Property owned by couples in community property states is divided loosely into two categories: separate property and community property.

Important Note

At the date of writing there are nine community property states: Arizona, California, Idaho, Louisiana, Nevada, New Mexico, Texas, Washington, and Wisconsin. In Alaska, couples can opt to have their property treated as community property under the terms of a written property agreement. The property distribution rules in these states may also apply to registered domestic partners.

A spouse's separate property is all property acquired by that spouse before he or she got married and after a divorce or legal separation, plus all property received as a gift or an inheritance and maintained separately (i.e. not jointly with his or her spouse) during that marriage. Community property, on the other hand, is all other property earned or acquired by either spouse during the marriage.

Separate property can also be deemed community property where it is formerly transferred by one spouse to the joint names of both spouses. Similarly, where property is gifted to one spouse and subsequently commingled with community property, the property can become community property.

Each of Alaska, Arizona, California, Nevada, Texas and Wisconsin allow a surviving spouse or domestic partner to automatically inherit community property when the other spouse or partner dies provided that property's title document makes it clear that the property is owned as community property with a right of survivorship in favor of the surviving spouse.

Normally, classifying property as community or separate property is relatively straightforward. However, there are several instances in which the classification is not clear. These include the ownership of businesses, companies, pensions, the proceeds of certain lawsuits, and incomes received from separate property. In cases such as these, you should consult a local attorney to determine how your state treats these items.

Most community property states do not grant a surviving spouse a legal right to inherit from the deceased spouse's estate. Rather, what they do is try to divide the marital assets (or registered partnership assets) during the lifetime of the spouses (or partners) by classifying certain assets as community property. Each spouse (or partner) in turn is deemed to own 50 percent of the community property.

However, in each of Alaska, California, Idaho, Washington and Wisconsin, a surviving spouse or domestic partner may elect to receive a specific portion of the deceased spouse's community or separate property in limited circumstances. For more information on such entitlements, we recommend that you consult a lawyer.

Warning

If you are in a registered domestic partnership and considering a move to another state, you should pay close attention to the laws of the state into which you are proposing to move as the "new state" may not recognize the property rights which you had in your "old state." If you are in any doubt as to how the law will affect you, you should consult a practicing lawyer in your area.

Common Law States

In common law states, each spouse owns all property acquired using their own income and all property legally registered solely in their name. Any property, such as your marital home for example, registered in the names of both spouses is deemed owned jointly. If you reside in a common law state, your spouse has a legal right to a fraction of your estate upon your death. Depending on which state you reside in, this legal right will usually amount to between one-third and one-half of your estate. The precise amount to which your spouse is entitled will also depend on whether you have any minor children and whether your spouse has been provided for outside the terms of your will or living trust.

The legal right of your spouse will take priority over any gifts made in your will or your living trust and will rank in priority after creditors of your estate. Your spouse will be entitled to either exercise his or her legal right to receive the specified fraction of your estate which he or she is entitled to or waive that right in favor of whatever has been left to him or her under the terms of your will and/or living trust.

The right of your spouse to take a defined percentage of your estate does not arise by the operation of law; rather it must be proactively elected. This means that your spouse must "speak up" and state that he or she wishes to exercise this right rather than accept what has been left to him or her under the terms of your will or living trust. Such election should be in writing and signed by your spouse. If your spouse fails to elect to take his or her legal share within the time frames set out under law, then he or she will be obliged to accept the gifts you have left to him or her under your will and/or living trust. Separately, your spouse can also waive his or her rights to this entitlement if he or she wishes.

Matters in relation to elections of a legal right can become more complex when a couple moves from a common law state to a community property state. In California, Idaho, Washington and Wisconsin, property acquired prior to a move will be treated as if it had been acquired in the state to which you have moved. In other community property states, the property will be treated in accordance with the laws of the state in which it was acquired. This can result in marital property being subjected to both common law and community property rules. In such cases, it is important that care is taken to determine which laws affect what types of property before you commence making your will or transferring property to your living trust.

By contrast, couples that move from a community property state to a common law state come up against the opposite problem. In such cases, each spouse retains a 50 percent interest in the community property acquired while the couple was resident in the community property state.

In addition to a surviving spouse's entitlement to claim a defined portion of their deceased spouse's estate, they also have several additional entitlements which we will discuss later in this chapter.

Gifts to Minors

Depending on your state's laws, minor children may only receive a nominal amount of property in their own names under the terms of a will, living trust or otherwise on a person's death. The amount varies from state to state but is usually between $1,000 and $10,000. If you leave a gift to a minor in excess of the permitted statutory amount, it will be necessary—either by the terms of your will, trust, or by a court order—to appoint a custodian, trustee or property guardian to manage those assets on behalf of the minor child. For more information on property management for minors, refer to Chapter 2.

Gifts to Charities

We all know of numerous charities that raise proceeds for a variety of good causes. In raising these proceeds, charities rely on the generosity of corporate sponsors and members of the public. Without this funding, many charities would simply not be able to carry on the valuable work they are doing. Accordingly, while you will naturally want to make appropriate provision for your family and friends in your estate planning documents, you may also want to make a gift (or at least consider doing so) to your favorite charity as well. This can be easily done under your will or living trust.

Making a gift is simple. All you do is identify the gift you wish to make and the charity that will receive the gift. As with any other beneficiary under your will, you can gift money or specific items, or nominate the charity as a beneficiary of the residuary of your estate or trust estate—the choice is yours.

However, where you choose to make a gift to a charity it is important to ensure that you provide clear details of the charity to be benefited. In this respect, it is useful to identity the charity by reference to its correct legal name (as it may differ from the "trading name" commonly used by the charity) as well as its charity registration number.

It is worth mentioning that several states impose limitations on leaving large portions of your estate to charity. Therefore, it is advisable to consult a lawyer if you wish to leave 50 percent or more of your estate to a charitable institution or a not-for-profit organization.

Failed Gifts

If you decide to gift a specific item to a beneficiary and you or the trust (as the case may be) subsequently dispose of the item before your death then, upon your death, the gift will fail because it cannot be completed. Where the gift fails, the intended beneficiary will not be entitled to receive a substitute gift unless you have expressly provided for this in your will or living trust. Additionally, if you gift a specific item or a particular amount of money to a named person and that person predeceases you, then unless an alternate beneficiary is entitled to receive that gift under the terms of your will or living trust, the gift reverts to form part of your residuary estate or residuary trust estate, as the case may be.

Imposing Conditions on the Receipt of Gifts

In making a gift under your will or living trust, you may wish to provide that the beneficiary will only be entitled to receive that gift if certain conditions are satisfied. While this is perfectly acceptable, it can be somewhat difficult to police.

There are two basic types of conditions that can be imposed on a beneficiary — conditions precedent and conditions subsequent.

A condition precedent is a requirement that must be met before the beneficiary is entitled to receive a gift. For example, you may specify that, "I give the sum of $5,000 to my nephew John Doe if he has obtained a college degree in engineering before December 31, 2025. If my nephew John Doe has not obtained the college degree as aforesaid, then I give the sum of $5,000 to my niece Jane Doe instead." The imposition of such a condition does not pose too many difficulties for the executor or trustee, as it will be easy to determine whether the beneficiary has met the requirement or not—although he or she may have to wait a while to find out. If the beneficiary fails to meet the requirements, then the proceeds being held by the executor or trustee to make this gift will be given to the alternate beneficiary or the persons entitled to the residuary interest in the estate or trust estate.

A condition subsequent, on the other hand, is a requirement that must be met after the beneficiary receives the gift. These types of conditions cause a lot more problems than conditions precedent because often the gift is received on the condition that the beneficiary fulfils an obligation, or a specific event occurs. Of course, problems arise where the obligation is not fulfilled, or the event never occurs.

If we took our example above and modified the condition such that it became a condition subsequent, it would read something like this: "I give the sum of $5,000 to my nephew John Doe on the conditions that he uses this money to obtain a college degree in engineering before December 31, 2030. If my nephew John Doe has not obtained the college degree as aforesaid, then I give the sum of $5,000 to my niece Jane Doe instead." In this instance, John has received the gift before he has satisfied the condition. This of course can be problematic. What happens if John fails to satisfy the condition within the required time frame? Well, Jane Doe will need to try and recover the $5,000 from John. Of course, this may be easier said than done.

While most conditions placed on the receipt of a gift are generally valid, there are some conditions that courts will refuse to enforce. Typically, these are conditions that are void for uncertainty (i.e. they are unclear) or void on the grounds of public policy. Conditions void on the grounds of public policy would, for example, include requirements that the beneficiary marry or refrain from marrying someone, divorce, or refrain from divorcing someone, change religion, or even murder someone.

A common restriction placed on beneficiaries comes in the form of a no-contest clause in a will or living trust. Under a no-contest clause, any beneficiary who challenges the will or living trust can lose all his or her right to inherit under that instrument. Without this clause, if a beneficiary is unhappy with their gift, they can sue the estate or trust estate and still be entitled to receive their original gift afterwards even where they lose—and by that time, the estate will have decreased in value because it will have had to incur legal fees and costs in defending the action.

Disinheritance

While the laws vary slightly from state to state, it is generally only a spouse that has any real entitlement to inherit from a deceased person's estate after they die. Understandably, many people are surprised to learn that children do not automatically have a right to inherit from their parents.

For one reason or another, many people consider disinheriting family members—often because of some underlying dispute. It is therefore important to look at how the laws work in this area so that you can, if you so wish, disinherit family members to the fullest extent permitted by law. We will do just that in the ensuing pages.

Disinheriting a Spouse

As discussed above, the laws of most states allow a surviving spouse the choice between what he or she has been left under the terms of his or her deceased spouse's will or receiving a specific share of the deceased spouse's estate as defined by statute. This share is known as the minimum or "elective" share. While the amount of this share tends to vary from state to state, the general rule is that if a deceased spouse had no children the surviving would be entitled to half of the deceased spouse's net estate. On the other hand, where the deceased spouse had children, the surviving spouse would have an entitlement to claim one third of the deceased spouse's net estate. Some states also impose financial thresholds. For example, under New York law, a surviving spouse is entitled to $50,000 or one third of the deceased spouse's net estate, whichever is the greater.

Did You Know ?

Divorce terminates the right of election by the surviving spouse.

Where the deceased spouse leaves more than the elective share of the net estate to the surviving spouse, the surviving spouse will generally not exercise the right of election unless he or she believed that it would be more advantageous to allow a greater part of the deceased spouse's estate to pass to the other beneficiaries named in the deceased's will, for tax reasons or otherwise. Of course, the surviving spouse's right of election is only valuable where the deceased spouse left less than the elective share to the surviving spouse. Consider, for example, the situation where a husband dies leaving everything to his children and nothing his spouse. In such a case, under New York law the surviving spouse would have the right to receive the elective share (i.e., the greater of $50,000 or one-third of the estate) notwithstanding the terms of the deceased spouse's will or living trust. The consequence of this is that the amount of the deceased spouse's estate passing to the children would be reduced. It may even be the case that certain beneficiaries no longer receive a gift under the deceased spouse's will.

If a surviving spouse elects to take his or her legal share rather than take what was left to him or her under the terms of the deceased spouse's will, then he or she generally forfeits the right to receive anything under the will. However, in many cases where an election is made, the surviving spouse will often be allowed take some or all of the specific items (depending on what was gifted to the surviving spouse) left to him or her under the will, particularly in circumstances where the amount left under the will is in fact less than the spouse's elective share. The balance of any amount owing to the surviving spouse is often then made up in cash. Alternatively, he or she can take assets from the residuary estate until the legal share is satisfied. On the other hand, if the spouse elects to take his or her inheritance under the deceased spouse's will, he or she will normally be entitled to receive those assets from the estate.

Whichever choice a surviving spouse makes, it's important to remember that they will (unless the terms of the will provides otherwise) still be entitled to avail of their other legal rights which, depending on the state law, include the right to buy certain estate assets, to remain in the principal residence for a specific period of time (usually a year), to claim and receive an allowance for their support, to receive automobiles and watercraft owned by the deceased, and to avail of such other rights as a surviving spouse would ordinarily be entitled to under law.

In most cases, the election of the surviving spouse will not affect certain non-probate property, such as jointly owned property and property with rights of survivorship attached such as pay-on-death accounts and transfer-on-death securities. However, the election may well effect other types of non-probate property, such as property held in a trust. That said, in states which have adopted the Uniform Probate Code, certain assets that have passed to the surviving spouse either during the life of the deceased spouse or on the death of the deceased spouse (through joint tenancy or on survivorship) are deemed part of the surviving spouse's elective share. You will need to check the laws of the deceased spouse's state of residence to determine what property is included in the surviving spouse's right to elect.

Did You Know

The Uniform Probate Code (the "Code") is a statute that unifies the laws governing the transfer of a person's estate. It deals with matters such as probate, transfers on intestacy, transfer of assets outside of probate, legal entitlements of spouses and trust administration. The Code was originally approved by the National Conference of Commissioners on Uniform State Laws and the House of Delegates of the American Bar Association in 1969. Its purpose was to modernize probate law and administration and to encourage uniformity in all fifty states. At the time of this writing, the UPC has been adopted by 16 states in full and by numerous states in part.

Uniform Probate Code — Full State Adoptions		
Alaska	Massachusetts	North Dakota
Arizona	Michigan	South Carolina
Colorado	Minnesota	South Dakota
Hawaii	Montana	Utah
Idaho	Nebraska	
Maine	New Mexico	

As you will have gathered from the foregoing, in most states the deceased cannot simply disinherit a spouse.

Disinheriting a Child

Unlike in other common law countries, in virtually every state in the United States it is possible to completely disinherit children. In fact, only in Louisiana is the ability to do so restricted. In order to disinherit a child, your will (as opposed to your living trust) must either (i) expressly state that you intend to disinherit your child, or (ii) make only a nominal gift to your child (such as a gift of $10). If you fail to adopt either of these two approaches and simply don't mention your child in your will at all, then you run the risk of your child challenging your will and a court subsequently making a determination that there has been an accidental disinheritance on your part. This could result in a re-distribution of your estate, with a large portion potentially going to your child.

If you wish to disinherit your child, it's best to include provisions similar to those mentioned in the preceding paragraph in both your will and your living trust, even where you have transferred all of your assets to your living trust.

Moreover, in some states the above laws apply not only to your children, but also to your grandchildren. This allows grandchildren to challenge the will of a grandparent who failed to provide for them or their dead parent. If your intention is to disinherit your grandchildren, it is important to ensure that your grandchildren are expressly disinherited in the same way as your children might be. Again, mention the disinheritance in both your will and living trust.

In certain circumstances, children are entitled to claim a share of a deceased parent's property regardless of the terms of the parent's will or living trust. For example, if you live in the state of Florida and are the head of your family for tax purposes, you will be prohibited from leaving your home to anyone besides your spouse or children.

Matters Affecting the Distribution of Your Assets

Before you make any decisions on how you wish to distribute your assets, it's useful to be aware of a number of specific rights and events that can have an impact on how your assets are ultimately distributed. These include the following:

- Simultaneous death.
- Homestead allowance.
- Family allowance for support.
- The exemption for the benefit of the family.
- Right to remain in the family home.

- Right to receive the family residence.

- Right to receive automobiles.

- Right to reimbursement of a funeral bill.

- Abatement of assets.

- Disclaimed inheritances.

We will consider each of these further below.

Simultaneous Death

It is common in wills and trusts to insert what is known as "common disaster" or "simultaneous death" provisions. These types of provisions usually state that in order for your beneficiary to receive a gift under your will or trust, they must survive you for a specific period of time, usually 30 to 60 days, before they can inherit from you. These types of clauses are aimed at the situations where, for example, you might die in an accident in which one or more of your named beneficiaries are also mortally injured. If that beneficiary survives you, and there is no required survival period, he or she could be entitled to receive the gift immediately on your death and, in doing so, would be obliged to pay certain estate taxes—which could become owing at the time of your death. If that beneficiary were to die shortly after you, the beneficiary's heirs would in turn be entitled to receive the asset and may well be obliged to pay estate tax on the item for a second time in quick succession. The provisions are designed to avoid these types of multiple administrations and the payment of estate taxes on the same assets where one of your beneficiaries dies of injuries a few hours (or days) after you.

This common disaster provision is most commonly used between spouses and provides for the transfer of the deceased's estate to the surviving spouse only if the surviving spouse survives the deceased spouse for a certain period of time following the deceased spouse's death. If the surviving spouse does not survive the deceased spouse for the requisite time frame, the assets will most usually pass to children or to other named beneficiaries under the will.

Homestead Allowance

In all states, a surviving spouse is entitled to a cash allowance from the deceased spouse's estate known as a homestead allowance. The amount of the allowance varies from state to state. In some states, the amount is fixed while in other it is dependent on the value of the deceased spouse's estate.

The states which have adopted the Code typically allow for an allowance of $27,000, as this is what is recommended under the Code. However, as the Code gives discretion to each adopting state to determine the precise amount of the allowance, it does vary substantially from state to state. For example, the allowance in Idaho is $50,000.

Under the Code, if your spouse predeceases you then each of your minor and dependent children is entitled to a pro-rata share of the homestead allowance (the relevant statutory amount, divided by the number of your minor and dependent children).

The homestead allowance is in addition to any share of your estate passing to your surviving spouse or minor or dependent children under your will (unless otherwise provided in your will), by intestate succession, or by way of elective share. It is also exempt from and has priority over all claims against your estate.

Family Allowance for Support

While the law varies from state to state, surviving spouses and dependent children are generally entitled to a cash allowance from a deceased spouse's estate for their maintenance during the period of probate administration. Under the Code, for example, they are entitled to a reasonable amount having regard to their previous standard of living and any other financial resources available to them. In other states, the amount tends to be a fixed monitory sum, such as in Florida where the amount is $18,000. The allowance itself may be paid as a lump sum or in periodic installments throughout the probate process.

You will need to check the laws of your state to determine the precise level of allowance available to your family.

The Exemption for the Benefit of the Family

In addition to the above rights, a surviving spouse is entitled in some states to certain property from the deceased spouse's estate (subject to certain monetary limitations) irrespective of whether the deceased spouse's will gives that property to them or not.

For example, in the states that have adopted the Code, the property to which a surviving spouse is entitled includes household furniture, automobiles, furnishings, appliances and personal effects not exceeding $10,000 in value. If there is not $10,000 worth of such property in the estate, the spouse is entitled to other assets of the estate, if any, to the extent necessary to make up the $10,000 threshold. If there is no surviving spouse, the deceased's children are entitled jointly to the same $10,000 benefit.

Right to Remain in the Family Home

A surviving spouse generally has the right to remain in the family home, if it is a probate asset, for a period of up to one year from the date of death of the deceased spouse. In some states, this period is extended to a right to remain in the family home for life. This applies notwithstanding that the house may have been gifted to someone else under the terms of the deceased spouse's will. However, if it happens that the family home is sold during the administration process to pay debts of the estate, the surviving spouse may be entitled to receive an amount from the estate equal to the fair rental value of the property as compensation for the loss of the right of residence.

The election of the right to remain in the family home must be made by the surviving spouse within a specific time frame following the initial appointment of an executor of the deceased's estate or else the right lapses. You should check the laws applicable in your state to determine the precise time frames in this respect.

Right to Receive Family Residence

In certain states, depending upon the value of the property, a surviving spouse may have the right to obtain the family residence as part of their inheritance. Moreover, a spouse may also have the right to purchase certain assets of the probate estate at the appraised values.

Right to Automobiles

In several states, a surviving spouse and/or children may be entitled to receive automobiles from the deceased's estate notwithstanding that they were not left to them under the terms of the deceased's will. In some cases, these assets fall under the entitlement referred to above as being "for the benefit of the family." Again, where applicable, this right needs to be exercised within the specific time frames set out under state law.

Right to Reimbursement of Funeral Costs

In some states, a spouse may be entitled to reimbursement by the deceased spouse's estate for the payment of the deceased's funeral costs.

Abatement of Assets

When the cash contained with the residuary of an estate is insufficient to pay the debts and taxes owing by an estate, it will become necessary to use some of the other assets of the estate to meet these payments. The process by which these assets are applied to pay the debts of the estate is known as "abatement."

Generally, the first assets of an estate to be abated are the cash reserves earmarked for the payment of legacies (i.e. the cash gifts). For example, if the estate has $50,000 in the bank account to cover cash gifts to the deceased's family and friends, and there are still debts owing by the estate after all of the residuary estate has been applied to meet those debts, then that money may be used to help discharge those debts. Any of the $50,000 remaining after payment of the debts in full will be distributed pro rata to the beneficiaries. However, if there insufficient cash funds to pay off all of the debts, then the executor can begin to sell the items left as specific item gifts (i.e. antiques, jewelry, real estate, etc.) in order to raise more cash to meet the debts. There are specific orders in which the gifts can be sold, and you will need to check the order which applies in your state for further clarification.

As you will have gathered, the net result following the abatement process is that people who have been left gifts under your will may not receive anything if the estate has high levels of debt. As such, in formulating your estate plan, you need to carefully consider the debt levels of your estate and even designate which assets you would like sold to meet those debts if there are insufficient cash reserves in the estate to meet the payments.

Disclaimed Inheritances

A beneficiary can renounce or disclaim their entitlement to receive a gift under a will or trust. This may be done, for example, because the gift is unwanted, the gift carries ongoing liabilities such as property maintenance, for tax reasons, or because the intended beneficiary simply wants to pass the gift to another beneficiary. If an alternate beneficiary has been named in your will or trust to receive that gift, he or she will then become entitled to it. If no alternate beneficiary is named, the gift will be passed to the beneficiary or beneficiaries entitled to the residue of the estate.

Finalizing Your Plan

Before finalizing your estate plan, it is important to talk with your family. One good reason for this is that it can often help resolve many potential disputes and worries before they arise. The perspective of a spouse or respected family member or friend who knows you well may help you reach decisions that you would not have reached on your own. Often, two (or more) heads are better than one.

Also, as difficult as it can be at the time, it is better to clear the air and bring things out in the open. By expressing your intentions regarding your property and sentimental distributions, you prepare your beneficiaries and those who will not be beneficiaries for what to expect following your death.

Family discussions are also useful in detecting and later planning to defend or divert possible challenges to your will or living trust. After you have discussed your estate plan and assessed your family's reaction to it, it will be imperative to ask yourself, "Is there any realistic likelihood of anyone challenging my will or living trust?"

Ordinarily you should have nothing to worry about, but there are scenarios of which you should be aware and of which you should keep in mind.

Lawsuits by Spouses

If you do not leave your spouse an appropriate amount of your property, he or she may have a legal right to claim their elective minimum share or even bring a lawsuit against your estate or trust estate to claim their lawful inheritance. This will no doubt be one of the most difficult things to discuss with others, but there may be benefits to talking about it with certain people in your family or friendship circles. It may be appropriate to explain to your spouse the reasons behind the insufficiency of the gifts being made to her.

Disinheriting Your Children

As with Dame Roddick, some people do not wish to leave much (or indeed anything) to a particular child or children. Technically, children have no right to inherit anything from their parents, but there are exceptions, and a surprised and disgruntled child may try to find those exceptions. More often, a disinherited child may feel they have been unintentionally overlooked and seek to "remedy the mistake."

It is felt by many that the best way to handle the sensitive matter of disinheritance is to leave some small amount to the child rather than nothing at all. Others recommend that the parents document the reasons for disinheriting their child in their will. If a small amount of money is left, you may insert a no-contest clause and state your reasons for the minimal bequest. In any event, if disinheritance is the path you feel you should follow, it is strongly suggested that you seek professional legal help. In addition, it is recommended that you discuss your intentions with other family members, who may be able to give you some helpful feedback.

CHAPTER 4

Last Will and Testament

About Wills

A will, more formally known as a "last will and testament," is a legal document that expresses your desires and intentions regarding the distribution of your real and personal property following your death. Real property is generally immovable property such as real estate, homes, land, and land improvements. Personal property, on the other hand, includes your movable property such as stocks, bonds, jewelry, furniture, clothing, artwork, etc. Basically, it is your will that determines how, when, and even why you want this property apportioned between your relatives, friends, and charities. In most cases, your heirs must honor the instructions set out in your will regarding the distribution of your property.

In addition to the distribution of your property, your will also appoints one or more people to act as your executor. Your executor will be charged with the task of carrying out the instructions set out in your will and winding up your affairs generally following your death.

Did You Know ?

Historically, a "will" document was used to transfer real property following a person's death, while a "testament" document was used to transfer personal property. However, the two documents merged over time to become a single document known as a "last will and testament".

Without a will, the decisions as to how your estate will be distributed and who will act as executor will be made by a court in accordance with your state's intestacy laws (i.e. the laws that apply where a person dies without a valid will).

As author of your will you are known as the "testator" as you are "attesting" to your wishes as set out in your will. The term "testator" has become gender neutral over the years and as such it refers to both male and female will makers. That said, it is not uncommon to see the female designation of the word ("testatrix") used, particularly in older wills.

Principal Components of a Will

Standard wills typically contain the following clauses:

- **Preamble*** — sets out the name and addresses of the testator.

- **Revocation*** — revokes all previous wills and other testamentary documents made by the testator.

- **Executor*** — appoints a person (or persons) known as an executor(s) (or a personal representative) to wind up the testator's affairs following his or her death.

- **Survivorship** — a common clause that requires beneficiaries under a will to survive the testator by a fixed period, such as 30 days, before they become entitled to inherit under the testator's will. This clause is commonly used in connection with gifts made by one spouse to the other and serves as a means of reducing multiple estate administrations and the possible double payment of estate taxes in respect of the same assets.

- **Cash gift** (legacy) — makes a gift of cash.
- **Specific property gift** (bequest) — makes a gift of a specific item of property.
- **Residue*** — makes a gift of all assets passing through the residuary estate to one or more beneficiaries.
- **Estate administration and expenses** — specifies how the testator's estate is to pay the debts, expenses, taxes, and costs of estate administration.
- **UTMA and child trusts** — creates a type of trust to manage property gifted to minor beneficiaries under the terms of the testator's will.
- **Guardianship** — appoints guardians and successor guardians to care for the testator's minor children.
- **Executive powers*** — sets out the powers to be granted to the executor(s).
- **Executors' fees** — states whether the executor(s) should be compensated for their work. Also specifies whether the executor(s) should be held liable in the event of incurring a loss of estate funds.
- **Attestation*** — the place where the testator signs and executes the will.
- **Witnessing*** — the place where the witnesses (usually two) sign and attest that they have witnessed the testator sign the will.

These items should appear in every will.

Types of Wills

There are many different types of wills in use today. Some wills, such as simple wills and testamentary trust wills, are recognized as legal in all states, while others are not. You will need to check with your attorney or check your state laws to see which types of wills are valid in your state. The main types of wills in use today are described below.

Simple Wills

This is the most common type of will made in the United States. It usually only provides for the distribution of an estate, the appointment of an executor and, if required, the appointment of guardians for minor children.

Testamentary Trust Wills

This is a will that provides for the establishment of a trust upon the death of the testator. On the testator's death, certain or all his or her assets will be transferred into a trust which will thereafter be administered by trustees appointed under the will in accordance with the terms of the will. This type of will is often used to provide for a spouse or young children.

Pour-Over Wills

A pour-over will is most used with trusts, such as living trusts. It is designed to transfer some or all the testator's assets to a trust fund following his or her death. The trust fund, in turn, will provide for the management and/or distribution of those assets. Unlike testamentary trust wills, these trusts are not created upon the testator's death, nor are their terms contained within the will document itself. Rather, these trusts are created before the testator dies under a separate trust deed or agreement. The most common example of a trust of this type is a living trust.

Self-Proving Wills

Normally, a will is presented to the probate court as part of the probate process. If there is any doubt as to the authenticity of the signature of the testator appearing on a will, the court may call upon the persons who witnessed the execution of the will to certify in court that the signature of the testator appearing on the will is in fact authentic and that the will was validly executed. One way of avoiding having to call these witnesses to court is to pre-validate the testator's signature. To do this, both the testator and the witnesses sign a document called an "affidavit." This is little more than a document in which the witnesses acknowledge that they witnessed the testator sign the will. However, importantly, it is signed in the presence of a notary who in turn officially seals the document to give it authenticity. The court will normally accept the execution of a will with an accompanying affidavit as genuine. The affidavit, when attached to the related will, is generally called a "self-proving will."

Holographic Wills

Holographic wills are wills that have been written in the testator's own handwriting. However, unlike most other wills, they do not need to be witnessed. This type of will is not valid in every state and, even where they are valid, we generally recommend that you avoid using them unless necessary under the circumstances.

Oral Wills

As the name suggests, this is a will that is verbally spoken rather than written down on paper. Very few states recognize the validity of such wills, and of those that do, most only recognize an oral will to be valid where it is made during a final illness and in respect of personal property that has a relatively low monetary value.

Joint Wills

A joint or mutual will is a single document incorporating the instructions of any two people, usually spouses, in relation to the disposal of both of their estates. The big problem with joint wills is that once one of the testators dies, the terms of the will cannot be changed. This means that the surviving testator is bound by the distribution provisions set out in the will. He or she cannot change it even where their circumstances have changed, and a change is warranted. We do not recommend the use of joint wills and suggest the use of two separate wills in its place.

Mirror Wills

A mirror will is a will that mirrors the provisions of another will. These types of wills are most used by a husband and wife (or partners) who wish to make almost identical provisions in relation to the distribution of their estates. For example, they may well wish to leave everything to the other if they die or, if both die together, to named beneficiaries (usually children). Unlike joint wills, each spouse or partner is free to change their will at any time, even following the death of the other spouse or partner.

Living Wills

Despite its name, this really is not a will in the normal sense. For example, unlike normal wills, which come into effect from the date of death of the author, a living will applies while the author is still alive. Also, while normal wills tend to dispose of property, the effect of a living will is to let doctors and hospitals know whether the author wishes to receive life sustaining medical treatment if he or she is suffering from a terminal illness or is in a state of permanent unconsciousness. Living wills, in varying degrees, are valid in all states.

Making a Valid Will

While most state laws do not require a specific will format, all state laws set out the minimum requirements for a will to be valid.

In general, for a will to be valid, it must:

- be made by a person who has reached the age of majority in his or her state (there are some exceptions to this general rule which we will discuss below).

- be made by a person voluntarily and without pressure from any other person—for this reason, it is not advisable for a potential beneficiary to be present when you instruct your lawyer to draw up your will or indeed to leave any gifts to your lawyer if he or she has drafted your will.

- be made by a person who is of "sound and disposing mind".

- be in writing (normally).

- be signed by the testator in the presence of two witnesses or, in the case of wills executed in the state of Vermont, three witnesses.

- be signed by all the witnesses in the presence of the testator (after he or she has signed it) and in the presence of each other (a beneficiary under the will or the spouse of such a beneficiary should not act as a witness to the signing of the will. If such a beneficiary or the spouse of such a beneficiary act as a witness, the gift to the beneficiary under the will shall be deemed to be invalid, although the will itself will remain valid).

- include an attestation clause.

- be notarized if made in the state of Louisiana.

Age of Majority

The age of majority is a legal description that denotes the threshold age at which a person ceases to be a minor and subsequently becomes legally responsible for his or her own actions and decisions. It is the age at which the responsibility of the minor's parents or guardians over them is relinquished. Reaching the age of majority also has several important practical consequences for the minor. The minor is now legally entitled to do certain things which he or she could not legally do before. For example, he or she is now legally entitled to enter binding contracts, hold significant assets, buy stocks and shares, vote in elections, buy and/or consume alcohol, and so on. But more importantly from an estate planning perspective, the minor can now make a will.

It is a general rule in each state that a person must reach the age of majority in their home state before being entitled to make a valid legal will. For details of the age of majority in each state, see Chapter 2.

There are, however, some exceptions to this general rule. Typically, a person under the age of majority who is already married, or who has been married, is deemed of sufficient age to execute a will. Emancipated minors may also execute a will. An underage person who joins the military or is on active military service can also make a will, as can a seaman or naval officer at sea.

Lastly, and in addition to the above, a court can specifically authorize the making of a will by a minor on application by the minor's parents or guardians. This might be approved, for example, where a minor inherited a large amount of money, invented some innovative computer software, or created the next Facebook with some friends. In each case, if the minor is shown to be of a sound disposing capability and the move is deemed prudent, the court will usually consider granting approval for the making of a will by the minor.

Mental Capacity and Undue Influence

To make a valid legal will, you must typically be of sound and disposing mind and memory. While the meaning of "sound and disposing mind and memory" differs slightly from state to state, it is generally taken to mean someone who understands:

- what a will is.
- that they are making a will.
- the general extent of their property.
- who their heirs and family members are.
- the way in which their property will be distributed under their will.

It is important to note that you need to be of sound mind and memory when you execute your will, not immediately prior to your death. As such, if you end up suffering from any kind of mental impairment late in life such as dementia or Alzheimer's disease, or even from an addiction to drugs or alcohol, the court will look at your mental state at the time you executed your will in order to determine whether it was validly made. If it can be shown that you were not mentally impaired or under the influence at the time you executed your will, the court will most likely deem the will to be valid. If you are suffering from any such impairments, it is advisable that you visit your doctor on the day you execute your will (or even execute it in your doctor's presence) and have your doctor prepare a medical certificate stating that in his or her professional opinion you were mentally competent and lucid at the time you executed your will. These types of statements generally have a strong persuasive effect on the courts, which typically tend to concede mental lucidity in such cases.

Another form of mental incapacity comes under the heading "undue influence." Undue influence is the exertion by a third party in a position of trust or authority of any kind of control or influence over another person such that the other person signs a contract or other legal instrument (such as a mortgage or deed) which, absent the influence of the third party, he or she would not ordinarily have signed. A contract or legal instrument may be set aside as being non-binding on any party who signs it while under undue influence.

Claims of undue influence are often raised by sibling beneficiaries in circumstances where one sibling is bequeathed more from a parent than the others. In making your will, you must therefore be careful to avoid potential claims of undue influence where you leave more to one of your children than another. Any such suggestion would give an aggrieved beneficiary the opportunity to attack and try to overturn the terms of your will. To reduce the potential likelihood of such claims, it is often useful to document the reasons why you are leaving more to one child than another. Your note can then be attached to your will or at least kept with it.

A second scenario in which claims for undue influence are often raised arises where a testator uses a beneficiary's attorney to draft their will. In such circumstances, aggrieved beneficiaries will, in reliance on that very fact, often assert that the use of the beneficiary's lawyer was evidence of the control the beneficiary had over the testator and the pressure that the beneficiary put on the testator to make the provisions he or she did in the will.

Example of Undue Influence

John constantly visits his uncle Bryan, an 88-year-old retired business tycoon, in the nursing home. During his visits, John continuously urges Bryan to leave his vast business interests to him—to the detriment of Bryan's own children who do not visit as often as they should. John, knowing that Bryan is lonely and depressed, threatens to stop visiting him as he is clearly ungrateful for John's kindness and attention. John finally arrives at the nursing home with his lawyer, who has never met Bryan before. John remains present while Bryan instructs the lawyer to write a new will for him in which he purports to leave all his business interest to John.

Ideally, an ethical attorney should never agree to make a will in such circumstances. But it does happen. Therefore, it is always wise to get independent legal advice when you make a will.

Why Make a Will?

There is no legal requirement to make a will. However, even for a person with the simplest of circumstances, there are several benefits to having a will. A will:

- allows you to dictate, via clear instructions, how you want your debts settled and assets distributed following your death.

- allows you to choose a representative to wind up your affairs.

- allows you to appoint guardians to take care of your minor children.

- allows you to make property management arrangements to cater for young beneficiaries who will inherit under your will.

- assists in preserving or even enhancing the value of your estate through the incorporation of tax and/or estate planning techniques.

- gives you peace of mind by allowing you to organize your affairs in a manner that you see fit—this in turn gives you the security of knowing that you haven't left behind a legal and emotional nightmare for your family and friends.

If you do not make a will, a court will make all the above decisions for you in accordance with the provisions of state law. These decisions may not be in accordance with your wishes.

Executors

An executor is the person named in a will to carry out the administration of the deceased's estate in accordance with the provisions of that will. If the deceased failed to make a valid will, or where there is a partial intestacy, the court will appoint a person known as an administrator to wind up the affairs of the deceased in accordance with state intestacy laws.

As we are talking about wills in this chapter, we will focus on the role of executors rather than that of administrators—although in many respects the two roles are similar.

If you are making a will, you are free to appoint anyone you wish to act as your executor if they have reached the age of majority in your state. You can appoint a relative, a beneficiary under your will, a lawyer, or even a bank or professional trustee as executor—the choice is yours. It is also possible to appoint more than one person as your executor. Where more than one executor is appointed, these co-executors can act separately (each one with full authority to act on behalf of the estate) or they can be required under the terms of your will to act jointly, in which case both executors (or all executors, if there are more than two) must agree to a course of action before taking that action.

Upon your death, your executor will have the legal responsibility and fiduciary duty to handle, safeguard and distribute your property in accordance with the terms of your will. In addition, your executor will also be responsible for procuring the payment of any debts or taxes owing by you or your estate at the date of your death. These debts and taxes, if any, will be paid from your estate (using the assets of the estate) before the distribution of the remainder of the estate's property to the beneficiaries named under your will.

These states use the term "personal representative" instead of "executor"		
Alaska	Maine	North Dakota
Arizona	Michigan	South Carolina
Colorado	Minnesota	South Dakota
Florida	Montana	Utah
Hawaii	Nebraska	Wisconsin
Idaho	New Mexico	

Alternate Executors

When making your will, it is always a good idea to appoint one or more alternate executors. An alternate executor is someone who will perform the duties of the first named executor if they are unable or unwilling to act (for whatever reason). If the alternate executor is required to act, he or she will be bound by the same legal responsibilities and fiduciary duties as the original executor.

Overview of Executors' Duties

As previously mentioned, an executor is the person responsible for carrying out the instructions set out in a will and settling an estate. An executor's duties will usually include locating, collecting, assessing and managing the estate's assets; arranging for the discharge of debts and taxes owed by the estate; distributing cash gifts and specific item gifts in accordance with the terms of the testator's will; and entering into appropriate contracts to effect the transfer of real property from the estate to the relevant beneficiary named under the will.

It is also the executor's duty to report the testator's death to insurance companies, banks, and other institutions that might owe money to or hold money on behalf of the estate.

It is common for executors to also be named as trustees of a person's will. In this respect, the testator may establish a testamentary trust for the benefit of certain beneficiaries rather than giving money or assets directly to them. As a trustee, the executor will be responsible for protecting, preserving, and investing the trust assets until the time comes to vest those assets in the trust beneficiaries. This usually occurs when the trust beneficiaries reach a certain age or on the occurrence of a specified event.

We will discuss executor duties further in Chapter 5.

Who Should Be Your Executor?

Choosing an executor is one of the most fundamental tasks associated with making a will. Getting the choice right can mean the difference between a smooth administration on one hand and a tardy administration with unexpected delays and costs on the other hand. It is therefore important to take your time and make the correct choice. Typically, the characteristics to look for in a good executor include good common sense, excellent organizational skills, and integrity.

Of course, many people tend to choose their spouse, a sibling, an adult child, or a good friend as their executor. Others choose professionals such as a lawyer, accountant, or professional trustee. All are good choices provided that the person chosen is both competent and trustworthy.

Other things being equal, it will often pay to choose a family member or friend as executor for the simple reason that these people expect little (if any) compensation in return for their time, will respect your wishes, and are generally keen to process and finalize things as quickly as possible. However, keep in mind that the process can be quite administrative, and time is often of the essence. So, you should still ensure that you choose someone who is organizationally reliable and generally up to the task.

Important Note

If your chosen executor refuses the appointment, a court will appoint someone to fulfill the role and this person will become known as the "administrator c.t.a." (cum testamento annexo)—meaning an "administrator with the will attached."

It is not enough, however, to simply appoint someone who has all the hallmarks of a good executor. You must appoint someone who is willing to take on the role as it is always open for a person to refuse to accept the role despite being nominated in a will. In fact, many often refuse to act as executors because they are either too busy to take on the task or feel daunted by the prospect of doing so.

For this reason, once you have decided on who you would like to act as your executor, it is important that you discuss your choice with them before appointing them in your will. You will need to explain to your proposed executor the nature of his or her role and that it may not be a straightforward and easy process. If your nominee is willing to take on the task after you explain the role, then you are be free to formally appoint him or her under your will.

Executing a Will

State laws set out the formal requirements for executing a will. While these laws are similar in each state, you should still check the specific requirements applicable in your state. In general, however, a "best practice" guide for executing your will could be summarized as follows:

- While it is only a legal requirement in the State of Louisiana, you should write your initials, in the presence of two witnesses (in Vermont, you should have three witnesses), at the bottom of each page of your will, except the last (signature) page.

- Each of the witnesses should then, in your presence and in the presence of each other, initial each page next to where you just placed your initials.

- You should then insert the date on which you are signing the will in the space provided on the final page of the will.

- You should write your initials beside where you inserted the date.

- Each of the witnesses should then, in your presence and in the presence of each other, write their initials beside where you placed your initials (i.e. beside the date).

- You must then sign your ordinary signature, using a pen, in the space provided on the final page.

- Each witness must then, in your presence and in the presence of each other, write his/her name and address in the space provided on the final page of the will and then sign their name with their normal signature.

While the actual execution of your will should be relatively straightforward, there are several additional rules which you need to be aware of when executing your will. Specifically, you should be aware of relevant laws related to witnesses and notarization.

With respect to witnesses, they should be at least 18 years of age or older and should not be your spouse or a beneficiary under your will (or a spouse of such beneficiary), as this could nullify any gifts made to them in your will.

Notarization is only required in the State of Louisiana. However, although it is not required in any other state, it is still recommended. We have discussed the requirements for notarization above under the heading of self-proving wills, and as such will not repeat the information here.

Finally, once you have executed your will, remember to keep it in a safe place. You should also consider informing your executor or even a close family member or friend of the location of your will so that it can be located when needed.

Important Note

Generally, a will must be signed by you or by someone directed to do so on your behalf. Signatures may include marks, initials, a rubber stamp, a "nick-name" or even a former name.

Matters that Can Impact Wills

In drafting your will, it is important to understand that events will most likely occur in your lifetime which will give rise to a need to change the provisions of your will. These events may come around because of changes in the law, your financial circumstances, the value of your assets, and even in your preferences in relation to beneficiaries. If your will is not updated to address these changes, they can have significant unintended consequences—particularly with respect to the way your assets are ultimately divided amongst your family members.

Some typical changes in circumstances that can cause unintended consequences if not addressed include:

- birth of new family members.

- death of intended beneficiaries.

- significant changes in beneficiaries' circumstances.

- changes in your relationships (such as marriage or divorce).

- acquisition of new assets.

- substantial appreciation in value of existing assets.

- disposal or substantial depreciation in value or loss of certain existing assets.

Important Note

Generally, a will must be signed by you or by someone directed to do so on your behalf. Signatures may include marks, initials, a rubber stamp, a "nick-name" or even a former name.

People with sizeable estates (generally those with a value more than the estate tax threshold—see Chapter 11) also need to keep an eye on taxes. This is because wills are often used as a method for pre-tax planning, whether in isolation or as part of a broader tax plan. Any change in tax thresholds or the level of taxes could have a substantial adverse effect on the potential value of your estate if the terms of your will remain unaltered. It is therefore important to watch for these changes and react accordingly.

No-Contest Clauses

A "no-contest" clause is a clause in a will that is designed to threaten to disinherit a beneficiary of a will if that beneficiary challenges the terms of the will in court. Where the beneficiary challenges the will, or any provision in it, the clause triggers a complete and total disinheritance of the beneficiary. An example of a simple no-contest clause is set out below:

"If any person, whether or not related to me by blood or in any way, shall attempt, either directly or indirectly, to set aside the probate of my will or oppose or contest any of the provisions hereof, then any share or interest in my estate given to that person under my will shall be revoked and, in its stead, I give and bequeath the sum of one dollar ($1.00), only that, and no further interest whatever in my estate to such person."

The Code allows for no-contest clauses so long as the person challenging the will does not have probable cause to do so (e.g. where the will has been fraudulently altered).

Should you wish to disinherit a child or a grandchild, you should expressly state your intention to do so and include a no-contest clause in your will. Thereafter, if your will makes no further reference to your child (apart from the statement of your intention to disinherit), the will effectively disinherits your child.

Also, keep in mind that if you have a child born after your will has been made, then in order to disinherit them it will be necessary for you to make a new will or add a codicil to your existing will. If you do not do so, you run the risk of having your will successfully challenged.

Challenging a Will

A "will contest" or "will challenge" is a legal objection to a will that is usually initiated by a family member or close relative who feels cheated out of their rightful inheritance, and therefore wishes to challenge the validity of the will in court.

Generally, only your spouse, children, and in some cases grandchildren, have the legal right to inherit from your estate. As such, any challenges to your will are most likely to emanate from one or more of these parties. Any challenges to your will are likely to focus on one or more of the following assertions:

- that you lacked sufficient mental capacity to fully understand what you were doing in making your will.
- that you were subjected to undue influence from a family member or advisor.
- that your will has been fraudulently tampered with.
- that your will has not been properly executed or witnessed in accordance with the law; or
- that the challenger has not been properly provided for under the terms of the will.

If the challenger is ultimately successful, the court will order a re-distribution of your estate based on the determination of court or, where the will is deemed to be invalidly made, in accordance with the rules of intestacy.

Intestacy

When a person dies without a will, if their will cannot be located, or if their will is deemed false or invalid (for not meeting the statutory requirements set out above), it is called dying intestate. Every state has statutory rules governing who is entitled to receive a person's property if they die intestate. These rules are commonly known as the "rules of intestacy" or the "rules of intestate succession."

Quite often, the application of the rules of intestacy results in the distribution of a deceased person's property in a manner that they would not have wanted. This is because the rules set out a list of people (known as "heirs") who are entitled to receive shares in the deceased's property, as well as the order in which they are entitled to receive those shares.

Generally, the rule of thumb in an intestacy situation is that the first beneficiaries to receive the deceased's property are the surviving spouse and then the children of the deceased. However, if there is no surviving spouse or children, then the general rule of thumb is that the bigger the estate is, the more distant the relatives who inherit part of it. Such beneficiaries might include the deceased's parents, siblings, grandparents, nieces and nephews, cousins and so on. In those rare cases where no relatives can be found, the deceased's property will revert to the state treasury.

Important Note

A partial intestacy occurs where you fail to dispose of your entire estate under your will. In such a case, property not specifically disposed of under your will usually becomes the subject of intestate administration proceedings.

In addition to providing for situations where a person has died without making a will, intestacy laws also apply to situations where a person has failed to deal with all their property under the terms of their will. This is called a partial intestacy.

Partial intestacy commonly occurs where a will fails to include what is known as a residuary clause. A residuary clause simply provides that any of the deceased's property which has not been specifically gifted under the terms of their will is to be given to a named beneficiary or beneficiaries known as the residuary beneficiary/beneficiaries. A partial intestacy can also occur where the residuary beneficiary or beneficiaries die before the testator and no alternate beneficiaries are named to receive the residue of the estate in their place.

The Main Differences Between Dying "Testate" and "Intestate"?	
Testate	**Intestate**
There is a valid will.	There is no will, or the will is invalid.
The will has been signed by the testator.	There is no will, or the will is invalid.
The estate of the deceased is referred to as a "testate" estate.	The estate of the deceased is referred to as an "intestate" estate.
The person dealing with the winding up of the estate will be known as the "executor of the will" or as the "personal representative."	The person dealing with the winding up of the estate will be known as the "administrator of the estate."
The personal representative will need to file a petition for probate of a will & letters testamentary.	The administrator will need to file a petition for letters of administration.
The person named in the will acts as executor or personal representative.	The administrator will be appointed in accordance with the rule of priority set out under state intestacy law.
The people who receive gifts under a will are called "beneficiaries."	The people who receive distributions on intestacy are called "heirs" or "heirs-at-law."
The beneficiaries are named in the will.	The heirs are determined in accordance with the rules of priority set out under state law.

When your will is admitted to probate (the legal process of determining the validity of a will and settling the estate), or in the event it is disputed by your heirs, the court will need to satisfy itself that the will is valid. To this end, it will look at issues such as your age and mental capacity at the time you made your will, whether there might have been any undue influence, as well as the manner in which the will was signed and executed. If all these matters are in order, then the will should be admitted to probate.

However, there are situations where valid wills might not be admitted to probate. This typically happens where the will is not admitted to probate within the time frame set out by state law (usually 30 days following the death of the testator). When this is the case, there is a real risk that the court might declare the will null and void and order that the deceased's estate be distributed according to the laws of intestacy.

Apportionment and Distribution of Assets on Intestacy

While intestacy laws generally vary from state to state, this variance has been greatly lessened by the Uniform Probate Code (which has been adopted by 18 states in full and by numerous states in part). The Code provides a good example of the rules relating to the distribution of assets on intestacy. However, you should check your own state law for a more thorough understanding of the rules applicable in your state.

Important Note

The intestacy laws which will apply to the distribution of a deceased person's assets will usually be the laws applicable in the deceased's state of residence.

Under the Code, priority of inheritance is given to the following persons in the following order:

- Surviving spouse.

- Descendants (children, grandchildren, etc.).

- Parents.

- Descendants of deceased's parents (siblings, nieces, and nephews).

- Grandparents.

- Descendants of grandparents (aunts, uncles, and cousins).

Under the Code, relatives are each apportioned a certain percentage of the deceased's estate. These percentages are set out below.

Share of Surviving Spouse

The share of a surviving spouse is calculated as follows:

- A surviving spouse is entitled to the entire estate if neither the deceased's descendants (i.e. children, grandchildren, and great grandchildren) nor the deceased's parents have survived the deceased.

- If the deceased's parents survive but no descendants survive the deceased, the surviving spouse is entitled to the first $200,000 of the estate plus ¾ of anything exceeding that amount.

- If the deceased is survived by a spouse and descendants from that marriage only, the surviving spouse will take the first $150,000 of the estate plus ½ of anything exceeding that amount, plus all community property.

- If the deceased is survived by descendants from the marriage to the surviving spouse and by descendants from someone other than his or her surviving spouse, the surviving spouse takes the first $100,000 of the estate plus ½ of anything exceeding that amount, plus all community property.

Share of Descendants

- If the deceased's spouse does not survive the deceased and the deceased's descendants do, then the deceased's descendants take the entire estate.

- In some cases, if the deceased's child has predeceased the deceased, that child's surviving children will inherit their parent's share of the intestate estate. This is known as "per stirpes" distribution.

Share of Parents

- If the deceased is not survived by a spouse or descendants, his or her entire net estate passes to his or her parents equally or, if only one survives, to the survivor.

Share of Other Relatives

- If neither the deceased's spouse, descendants, nor parents survive the deceased, the entire net estate passes to the deceased's siblings. If there are no siblings or no descendants of the deceased's siblings, the deceased's estate goes to any surviving grandparents or their descendants.

Do-It-Yourself Wills

While you can easily obtain will forms and other legal document forms in a "fill-in-the-blanks" format online or from various stores, we recommend that you take extreme care in determining which forms to use and which to ignore. Your personal, financial, and other circumstances will grow in complexity as you age and, as such, your changing needs might not be sufficiently addressed by a "one-size fits all" form. This will apply particularly where you have a large estate such as one which exceeds the value of the current estate tax thresholds (see Chapter 11) or where you have complex business and financial interests.

However, if your estate is "normal" then, in many cases, these documents can suffice. For example, if a husband and wife wished to leave everything to each other in the event of their death, or if both died at the same time, to their children, a do-it-yourself will can suffice. This is because the distributions are relatively straightforward. Similarly, if you simply wish to make normal gifts (real estate, cash, art, etc.) to your family and friends, these types of wills are also generally fine.

Yet it can happen that the use of sub-standard do-it-yourself wills leads to confusion in the interpretation of your will, delays in distributions being made and unwanted tax consequences. In one well-known case, a do-it-yourself testator wrote: "I leave all my personal property to my wife." Endless chaos ensued because the law distinguishes "real property" (land and real estate) from "personal property" (all property other than land and real estate, but including leasehold property, such as cash, antiques, etc.). Here the bulk of the estate was in the form of freehold land, which on a literal reading was simply not dealt with under the will and could have been split between various relatives upon intestacy. In this case the widow had to go through the trauma, delay, and considerable expense of seeking a declaration that her husband intended her to inherit his real estate, as well as his personal estate. (The testator's personal estate in the case in point was not of great value.)

> # Warning
>
> While all EstateBee's legal documents are drafted to an extremely high standard, we have no way of knowing whether they are suitable for you under your circumstances. As such, you still need to use these documents with care as the decision to use them is up to you. If you are in any doubt as to their suitability for you, speak to an attorney.

If you are happy to draft a do-it-yourself will, we recommend that you carefully consider the use of such a document in the context of your overall situation and personal circumstances. Where you have any doubt or concern as to the suitability of a particular document to your circumstances, you should consult an estate planning lawyer before you sign. It is the best way to ensure you do not end up with messy, unintended consequences. The price you will pay for peace of mind—and the assurance that those you want to inherit will inherit—will be more than worth it.

Do I Need a Lawyer?

The short answer is "no." In every state, citizens are free to draft their will on their own, without legal representation. If your situation is not a complicated one, and you simply want to make gifts, appoint guardians and executors, etc. under your will, then preparing your own will should not be very difficult provided that you have some good self-help materials to hand. But as with the do-it-yourself kits, if your situation is complex or is unusual in some way, you should, at the very least, consult an attorney.

Resource

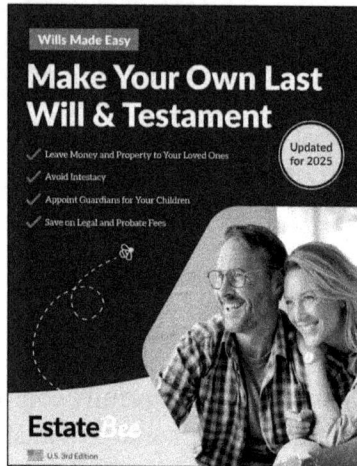

Make Your Own Last Will & Testament

By making a will, you can provide for the distribution of your assets to your loved ones, appoint guardians to care for your children, provide for the management of gifts to young adults and children, specify how your debts are to be paid following your death, make funeral arrangements and much more.

This book will guide you through the entire process of making a will. It contains all the forms that you will need to make a valid legal will, simply and easily.

Get your copy at www.estate-bee.com/product/make-your-own-last-will-and-testament/

CHAPTER 5

Executors & Probate

What Is an Executor?

An executor is a person appointed under a will for the purpose of winding up an estate and distributing the deceased's property in accordance with the terms of his or her will.

The role of executor is both important and difficult. Your executor must be prepared to carry out the sometimes wide-ranging, sometimes minimal, steps required to finalize every aspect of your estate. Often, the probate of your estate will require much more from your executor than simply writing checks and giving your beneficiaries their gifts from your estate. The process can be a demanding and time-consuming task involving complicated taxes, fee payments, disputes amongst beneficiaries, and tricky asset transfers. It is therefore important that you appoint an executor capable of navigating the sometimes-treacherous waters of probate and estate administration.

What Is Probate?

Probate is the process by which your property is transferred to the beneficiaries named in your will after your death, which is usually carried out under court supervision. If you have not made a will and die intestate, the comparable process is known as "intestate administration," which is guided by state law and entails court supervision.

Every state has its own set of probate laws (often codified in a probate code) which set out the specific rules and procedures for probate in that state. At a minimum, these laws typically stipulate the requirements for a valid will, tell us who is going to administer the estate, tell us who is entitled to receive assets from the estate, identify which creditors need to be paid upon the deceased's death and in what order of priority, and determine how to distribute the balance of the deceased's assets after the payment of all taxes and debts of the estate.

Each state has its own set of specific procedures which must be followed when bringing an estate to probate. In most cases, the procedure is the same. Generally, your executor's first task will be to locate your will, as without a will probate cannot take place. For this reason, it is recommend that upon appointing your executor you provide him or her with details of where your will can be located when the time comes (e.g. in a safe deposit box, in your lawyer's office, etc.). After locating your will, your executor should try to determine whether the will is valid "on its face" by ensuring, for example, that it has been signed by you and witnessed by the correct number of witnesses. Most states require a will to be witnessed by two witnesses (three in Vermont). Your executor must also determine that the located will is in fact your last will as only your last will has any legal effect.

Next, if your will is in legal order, your executor must determine whether probate is required and, if so, file your will in the probate court and apply for probate. This simply means that your executor sets in motion the process of legally proving the validity of your will and obtaining the consent of the court to wind up your affairs. Whether probate is required or not depends on the laws of your state. In some states, probate is required for all estates. In others, estates with a small monitory value will not need to go through the probate process or, alternatively, can avail of a more streamlined procedure for winding up the estate.

Once an application for probate has been made, it is the probate court's job to formally rule upon the validity of your will (quite often this is just a rubber-stamp affair). However, the court must wait a specific period before doing so to allow any challengers to your will (or part thereof) to file their objection. Any such challenges must be made within a specified timeframe (which changes from state to state, so your executor will need to check the notice and timing requirements for your state).

Once the court deems the will valid, and accepts your executor's appointment as executor, your executor may begin to pay taxes, settle debts and other claims against your estate and, when this is done, distribute the estate's assets to your beneficiaries. If the will is invalid, your executor will need to proceed as if you died intestate, in which case the court will appoint an administrator to administer the estate. This may or may not be the executor you have chosen in your will depending on state law.

Finally, the last step of the process occurs when your executor finalizes your estate by filing the necessary papers and accounts with the court. These must include: an accounting of assets that formed part of the estate; details of what was paid out from the estate (and why); and copies of any notices and tax returns issued, received or filed by the estate. Your executor will be expected to provide proof of distribution of your assets to the correct beneficiaries, usually by providing signed receipts from the beneficiaries. Also included may be copies of deeds signed by your executor for the transfer of real property, and instruments of distribution for any of your personal property.

As soon as the court recognizes that your executor has successfully completed all the steps necessary to administer your estate, he or she will be released from further service as executor and your estate will be closed.

Who Can Be Your Executor?

In practice, you are free to appoint anyone you wish to act as your executor—subject to a few exceptions. Normally, a person will not be able to act as an executor if they are under the age of majority in their state of residence, if they have been convicted of a felony, or are not a U.S. citizen.

In addition, certain states prohibit people residing outside that state from acting as executors unless insurance bonds are first put in place. As such, if you are planning on appointing an out-of-state resident as your executor, you should check your state laws to see if a bond is required. The cost of any such bond will be borne by your estate.

An Overview of an Executor's Duties, Powers and Risks

While it is not within the scope of this book to provide a comprehensive discussion of an executor's duties, it is useful for you to have a general understanding of those duties so that you can decide who is best for the role.

In essence, an executor will have two types of duties—procedural duties and fiduciary duties. Procedural duties are actions that the executor must perform to bring the estate through probate. Fiduciary duties, on the other hand, are duties that the executor owes to the beneficiaries of the estate whose assets the executor has control over.

Once the executor has applied for probate, he or she will have the following procedural duties and responsibilities:

- Notifying beneficiaries named in the will of their potential interest.

- Drafting and arranging publication in a newspaper of a notice to creditors and sending a copy of that notice (by mail) to each creditor that the executor knows of.

- Sending copies of the deceased's official death notice to the post office, utility companies, banks, and credit card companies.

- Locating and safeguarding assets.

- Inventorying assets and having them appraised and valued.

- Collecting all moneys owing to the estate.

- Checking with the deceased's employer for any unpaid salary and benefits that might be owing to the estate.

- Filing for outstanding social security, civil service, veteran, and other benefits.

- Filing claims for life insurance benefits.

- Filing state death tax and federal estate tax returns.

- Paying out valid and proven claims against the estate.

- Distributing all remaining assets to the beneficiaries.

An executor also owes your estate and its beneficiaries a fiduciary duty arising from his or her position as executor. A fiduciary duty arises where a person undertakes to act for and on behalf of another in relation to a particular matter and in circumstances which give rise to a relationship of trust and confidence between the parties. A fiduciary duty is a legal one and breach of that duty gives rise to a cause of action against the fiduciary (i.e. the executor).

The main fiduciary duties that your executor will have include the duty to:

- adhere strictly to the terms of the will and to your intentions.

- keep estate assets separate from other assets.

- keep accurate records and accounts of the estate's dealings.

- provide information to the beneficiaries named in your will in a timely manner.

- administer the estate with the same due care and skill that a person of ordinary prudence would exercise in dealing with his or her own property.

- administer the estate in the best interests of the beneficiaries and not in the executor's self-interest.

- avoid conflicts of interest, whether actual or perceived.

Powers of an Executor

Until termination of his or her appointment, your executor will have the same power over the title to your property as you would ordinarily have. However, this power is exercisable in trust for the benefit of your creditors and beneficiaries.

In addition, executors are afforded a variety of additional powers under state law. These include the power to:

- employ persons for the purpose of valuing assets and evaluating the liabilities of the estate.
- receive a defined level of compensation or a reasonable level of compensation in return for acting as executor of the estate.
- petition the court for an order determining the validity of a will, determining the entitlement of beneficiaries to claim under the will, approving the final accounting of the estate as prepared by the executor, and approving the plan of distribution of the estate assets.
- distribute the estate's assets.
- close the probate of the estate.

In addition to the powers granted under state law, executors tend to be afforded further powers under the terms of a will. These additional powers are given to the executor to allow him or her to manage the testator's estate. Typically, the larger the estate, the greater the extent of the powers given to the executor.

Executor's Liability

As with any position of responsibility, there are potential personal liabilities that come with the role of executor.

For example, your executor can be held liable (civilly and/or criminally) if he or she:

- violates any applicable law.
- fails to comply with the terms of your will.
- abuses any of his or her powers as executor.
- deals in the estate assets for his or her own account.

- causes unreasonable delay in administering the estate.

- causes loss, damage, or devaluation of any assets.

- acts without appropriate approval, including those actions that require the consent of the estate's beneficiaries, the prior approval of co-executors, or the prior approval of a court.

- fails to make any payment or secure any debt.

Further, while executors are empowered to seek advice before making investment decisions, the ability to make these decisions is personal to the executor and cannot be delegated. Any improper delegation of executor duties or responsibilities, such as allowing investment advisors complete discretion to make decisions on behalf of the estate's investments, can open the door to liability for both restitution and damages. If your executor is found guilty of a breach of his or her duties or responsibilities, the court can require the executor to compensate the estate for any loss suffered by it. The compensation amount is often referred to as a "surcharge."

Protecting Your Executor from Liability

If someone agrees to perform as your executor, you should see to it that they are protected from liability in return for their last, generous act of friendship. Below we describe several ways that you can ensure that your executor is protected. While some of these ways need to be provided for in your will, others need to be implemented before your death.

Protection Under the Terms of Your Will

The terms of your will can be drafted in a manner so as to reduce the chance of your executor being exposed to personal liability in circumstances where he or she acts diligently and in good faith in the carrying out of his or her duties. For example, your will could authorize your executor to manage a particular business activity that was somewhat risky and, in conjunction with doing that, could provide that the executor will not be held liable for any loss to the value of that business where he or she acts in good faith. The rationale for the inclusion of such clauses is relatively straight forward. In the absence of including these exclusion clauses, your executor would most likely abstain from taking on any involvement in the management of such assets in circumstances where he or she could find himself or herself being sued personally for any subsequent loss—even where the executor did all he or she could humanly do. These clauses allow executors to get on with the business at hand while at the same time ensuring that they still act with due care and attention in the performance of their duties.

Obtain the Consent of Beneficiaries

Another way in which your executor can reduce the possibility of personal liability is to obtain the written permission of all concerned beneficiaries before taking a particular course of action or the carrying out certain activities, for example the sale of real estate investments. This consent can be obtained by you before you die or by your executor after you die.

While it is not vital, the written consent should expressly state that the beneficiaries will not hold the executor liable if they carry out the approved action(s). The mere existence of such a written approval would make it exceptionally difficult for beneficiaries to subsequently take a successful action against the executor for losses to the estate incurred from the carrying out of the approved activities (unless of course the executor was negligent in carrying out the activities approved by the beneficiaries).

Take Out an Executor's Insurance Bond

One of the best protections available to executors is insurance coverage. The estate and/or the executor can take out executor insurance in the form of a surety bond, obtainable from most insurance companies. The bond protects both beneficiaries and creditors from losses suffered by the estate due to neglect or omission by the executor. Although a bond is not always required, beneficiaries or even the probate court may request one. While it protects the estate, it also protects the executor from personal liability as he or she is afforded monetary protection up to the value of the insurance bond. The value of the bond should, in most cases, equate to the full value of the estate. The premium for the bond will be payable by the estate.

You can expressly require the executor to take out such a bond under the terms of your will. The costs of the bond will be borne by your estate.

Obtain the Consent of the Probate Court

Finally, where an executor is uncertain as to how to proceed in a particular situation, he or she may apply to court for directions on how to proceed. Having considered the issue, the court will direct the executor on how best to proceed in the circumstances. This direction will be given in the form of a court order. Where the executor follows the directions of the court order to the letter, it would be extremely difficult for a beneficiary to act personally against the executor given that he is carrying out actions sanctioned by the court. However, if the court was not aware of all the facts in the case, the executor would not be adequately protected.

Compensating Your Executor

You can draft your will to pay your executor a fixed fee, an hourly fee, a statutory fee, or no fee at all. Should you choose a fixed or flat fee, you simply write that fee into the will in a compensation clause. Most states have a statutorily defined "reasonable rate of compensation" for executors (and trustees). This rate is sometimes a percentage of the net value of the estate, e.g. 2.5 percent.

Often, if you appoint a close friend, relative or family member, you can pre-arrange that they will serve their appointment for free. However, remember that probating an estate is a time-consuming and difficult task. Therefore, if possible, you may wish to compensate your executor, at least nominally.

If you draft your will to refuse or overly limit compensation to your executor, we recommend that you include an exemption for professional services, e.g. banks, lawyers, etc. Professionals most often will not serve without compensation and will therefore insist on charging their professional rates to the estate.

Resource

Probate Made Easy
How to Probate an Estate
A Step-by-Step Guide for Executors
Updated for 2025
✓ Deal with Creditors' Claims, Taxes & Trusts
✓ Learn How to Locate & Manage Estate Assets
✓ Initiate & Close Probate with Ease
✓ Avoid Common Executor Mistakes
EstateBee
U.S. 3rd Edition

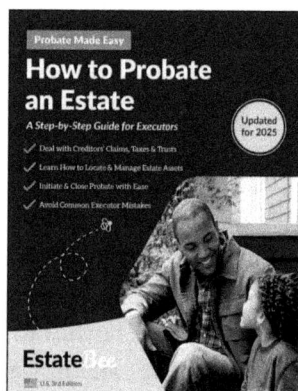

"How to Probate an Estate" is essential reading for anyone thinking about acting as an executor of someone's estate. It is designed to guide readers step-by-step through the entire probate process and to give them the knowledge and confidence to act as an executor.

It explores each step of the probate process from the moment the deceased dies right through to the distribution of the deceased's assets and the closing of the estate. It is a one-stop resource for successfully probating an estate.

Get your copy at
www.estate-bee.com/product/how-to-probate-an-estate/

CHAPTER 6 | # Powers of Attorney

What Is a Power of Attorney?

A power of attorney is a legal document by which you can appoint and authorize another person (usually a trusted friend, family member, colleague or adviser) to act on your behalf and to legally bind you in that respect. While most people fail to see the importance of having a power of attorney, there are many compelling reasons to have one. Suppose:

- you are going to be out of the country for an extended period and need someone trustworthy to manage your business affairs while you are away.

- you wish to acquire property in another state, and you need to authorize a local to sign and file documents on your behalf.

- you want someone to manage your real estate for you.

- you are getting a little bit older and wish to appoint someone you know and trust to make healthcare decisions on your behalf should the day come when you are unable to do so yourself.

A power of attorney can be used to facilitate your needs in each of these scenarios.

The person giving the power of attorney is referred to as the "donor", "grantor" or "principal", while the recipient is called the "agent", "attorney-in-fact" or just plain "attorney" (which doesn't mean they have to be a legal practitioner).

Types of Powers of Attorney

There are several different types of power of attorney, all serving different needs and requirements. We will look at some of the main types below.

General Power of Attorney

A 'general power of attorney' is virtually unlimited in scope. It allows your agent to act as your authorized legal representative in relation to the whole cross-section of your legal and financial affairs, until such time as that authorization is terminated. In other words, your agent will have full legal authority to make decisions and take actions on your behalf, as if you were taking them yourself. This could, for example, include signing letters and checks, executing contracts, opening, and closing bank accounts, and so on.

While you cannot generally limit the scope of the power conferred under a general power of attorney, there are nonetheless some presumed limits to the agent's authority. For example, your agent is not normally permitted to assume any position or office that you might hold. These offices would include positions as employee, company director, trustee, personal representative, and others. In addition to that, your agent cannot execute a will on your behalf (or amend an existing one), take action concerning your marriage or delegate his or her authorization under your power of attorney to a third party, unless expressly authorized to do so in the power of attorney document. An agent is also prevented from making gifts of your assets, other than small gifts that you yourself might have been expected to make having regard to the size of your estate.

Important Note

It is important to bear in mind that you will remain personally liable for the actions of your agent, so you should grant authorization only to someone you trust implicitly. Where you do grant authorization, you should monitor their actions appropriately. This applies in respect of all types of powers of attorney.

A general power of attorney (unless stated to be durable) automatically comes to an end if you become mentally incapacitated or die. It will also come to an end on any termination date set out in the document itself.

Limited Power of Attorney

A 'limited power of attorney' is like a general power of attorney except that it imposes specific and sometimes substantial limits upon the authorization granted to your agent. This could, for example, be a limit to the scope or duration of the authority granted to your agent.

Often, people granting powers of attorney limit their agent's authority to completing specific transactions or tasks. For example, you may appoint someone as your agent solely for the purpose of having them sign a document on your behalf but only in a format pre-approved by you and attached to the power of attorney document itself. Alternatively, you can appoint your agent for the sole purpose of dealing with a single task or transaction (such as the sale of a piece of real estate to a specified individual at a specified price and on specified terms). These types of limitations remove a substantial part of the risk associated with granting powers of attorney. The good news is that there are no limits on the limitations you can impose on your agent's authority. So, you can be as precise in the authority you grant your agent as you wish.

Like the position with a general power of attorney, you will remain personally liable for the actions of your agent.

The limited power of attorney will continue in force until it comes to an end on a date set out in the power of attorney document – assuming there is one. In any event, it will automatically come to an end if you become mentally incapacitated or die.

Healthcare Power of Attorney

One of the most common forms of power of attorney in use today is the "medical" or healthcare power of attorney).

A healthcare power of attorney allows you to authorize an agent to make healthcare decisions on your behalf if you are incapacitated and unable to make those decisions yourself. The authorization conferred on your agent can cover any form of healthcare decision. Unlike documents such as living wills, the agent's authority under a healthcare power of attorney can apply even where you are not terminally ill or permanently unconscious. So, for example, it could apply if you suffered temporary unconsciousness (if you were in an accident, for instance) or if you were suffering from a mental illness like Alzheimer's disease which affects the decision-making process.

Unlike general and limited powers of attorney, a healthcare power of attorney does not automatically terminate if you become incapacitated. Better still, you can even specify in your healthcare power of attorney document that your agent's authority only comes into effect if your physicians determine that you have become incapacitated or are otherwise unable to make decisions for yourself.

In your healthcare power of attorney document, you can specify guidelines and directions regarding the types of medical treatment you wish to receive during any periods in which you are unable to make healthcare decisions on your own behalf. Other than in the most extreme cases, your agent will be obliged to follow these instructions and direct your physicians to follow them. As an alternative to expressly specifying your wishes, you can also give your agent full discretion to make healthcare decisions on your behalf during any period in which you are unable to. Of course, be mindful who you give such authority to.

Ordinary and Durable Powers of Attorney

In addition to the three types of powers of attorney that we have just described, powers of attorney can also be categorized as either being 'ordinary' or 'durable'.

Ordinary powers of attorney are only valid for as long as you can make decisions on your own behalf. If you die, or become mentally incapacitated, your power of attorney immediately ceases to have effect and your agent's authority immediately comes to an end. If this happens, your family and business partners could be left in a situation where they are powerless to legally deal with your affairs without seeking court intervention. Some examples of typical problems include the inability to transfer real estate held in joint names, deal with bank accounts that require dual signatories, and the execution of legal documents generally.

Durable powers of attorney, on the other hand, remain valid even if you become mentally incapacitated. In fact, under many durable powers of attorney, your agent's authority to act only becomes effective if you become incapacitated. By giving a trusted family member, friend, or adviser authority to legally make decisions on your behalf while incapacitated, you can ensure that your family's interests and business interests are protected. Of course, like all powers of attorney, durable powers of attorney will come to an end if you die.

In a durable power of attorney that only becomes effective if you become incapacitated, it is usual to see a clause which provides that a doctor must personally examine you and determine that you are incapacitated and unable to handle your financial affairs before your agent's authority will come into effect. It is that determination that then acts as the trigger for your agent's authority to commence.

To be recognized as durable, your power of attorney must contain a clear and unambiguous statement to the effect that it is intended to be 'durable'. It is also helpful to include an express statement to the effect that 'this power of attorney shall not be affected by my subsequent incapacity' or that 'this power of attorney shall become effective upon my incapacity'. Statements of this type help make it clear that your power of attorney was intended to be durable and to be valid even if or after you became incapacitated.

Springing Powers of Attorney

A 'springing' power of attorney is one that becomes effective at a future time or on the occurrence of a future event. That event could include your incapacity or might be something as simple as the date upon which you complete the purchase of a piece of real estate, open a bank account, or otherwise. Springing powers of attorney can be general or limited, as well as ordinary or durable. They can even be healthcare powers of attorney.

Mutual Powers of Attorney

Mutual powers of attorney are usually made between a husband and wife, and occasionally between the members of smaller businesses or professional firms. They serve as indicators of the mutual trust, confidence, and reliance that the parties enjoy within their relationship.

Under these powers of attorney, each spouse or partner will appoint the other (or others) as their agent so as to ensure that their joint plans are implemented in the unfortunate event that one of them is rendered unable to act by illness or injury. For this reason, they are usually durable powers of attorney. As between a husband and wife, they are often durable general powers of attorney (which are unlimited in scope), whereas between business partners they are often durable limited powers of attorney (which, as the name implies, are limited in scope).

Cascading Powers of Attorney

A cascading power of attorney is simply a form of power of attorney which allows for the appointment of alternative or substitute agents. Its purpose is to provide for a backup in the situation where the first agent is unable or unwilling to act, and then further backups to replace the alternative agent if they also decline to act, or cannot act for any reason.

Capacity to Make a Power of Attorney

Generally, anyone who has reached the age of majority in their state of residence, who has sufficient mental capacity, and who is not an un-discharged bankrupt can make a power of attorney. Even a company or a partnership can make a power of attorney.

Having sufficient mentally capacity to make a power of attorney generally means that you must, at the time of making it, be aware of the nature and extent of your assets and personal circumstances, understand your obligations in relation to your dependents and understand the nature of the power being granted to your agent under your power of attorney.

The precise requirements for making a power of attorney differ from state to state. As such, if you are in any doubt as to whether you can make a power of attorney, you should seek the advice of a practicing attorney in your state.

What Does 'Being Incapacitated' Mean?

You will be deemed to be "incapacitated" if you are unable to understand and process information that is relevant to making an informed decision and if you are also unable to evaluate the likely consequences of making that decision.

The decision as to who determines whether you are incapacitated or not is generally set out in your power of attorney. Generally, a power of attorney will state that two doctors or attending physicians must agree that you are incapacitated before your power of attorney comes into effect.

While it may be somewhat obvious, it is worth pointing out that you must be mentally capable of granting a power of attorney at the time when the document was signed. This generally means that you must, if required, show that you are aware of the nature and extent of your assets and personal circumstances, and that you understand your obligations in relation to your dependents and the nature of the power being granted to your agent under your power of attorney.

If you are found to be incapacitated in a time where you believe you are not, you have the right to request a capacity review hearing for the purpose of affirming or quashing that determination. You will have the right to be represented by counsel at that hearing. Agents appointed under a power of attorney have a general duty to explain this right to you and cannot try to prevent you from contacting a lawyer or asking for a review hearing. This said, it should be remembered that unless the agent is a professional accustomed to acting under a power of attorney, the likelihood is that the agent will not be aware of his obligation in this regard.

Should I Make a Power of Attorney?

The simple answer is yes. If you have an income or property of any description, it's a good idea to execute a durable power of attorney— especially if you believe that health problems may make it impossible for you to handle your personal financial affairs in the future. Even if you have no impending health issues, you should still have a durable power of attorney in case you have an accident or sudden illness and become unable to make decisions for yourself.

Have you ever considered what would happen if:

- You were involved in a serious accident which left you in a coma. What would your family do, in both the short and the longer term, if they had no power to access your bank accounts or take care of your business affairs?

- You began to have blackouts and act in an out-of-character fashion. You are diagnosed as having a brain tumor, and before long you lose the capacity to function normally or make rational decisions. Will your property, financial and other affairs be stuck in limbo?

In both cases, a durable power of attorney would be of great assistance to you. During your period of incapacity, your agent would be able to manage the many practical and financial tasks that may arise. For example, bills will need to be paid, bank deposits will need to be made, and someone will need to handle insurance and benefits paperwork.

Many other matters may need attention as well, ranging from handling property repairs to managing investments or even a small business. In most cases, a durable general power of attorney is the best way to take care of all these and other similar tasks.

In addition, by preparing a power of attorney now, you can ensure that a person of your choosing will manage your property, assets, and affairs rather than a court appointed conservator.

What Happens Without a Power of Attorney?

If you do not make a durable power of attorney, someone may have to be formally appointed by a court to make financial and other practical decisions (other than medical decisions) on your behalf. Specifically, your family will have to make an application to a court to have it make a determination that you cannot take care of your own affairs and request the court to make an order appointing a "conservator" (also known as a "guardian of the estate," "committee," or "curator") on your behalf. This application is often made in public, and in some instances a notice of the intended application may even be published in a local newspaper. This can, as you will appreciate, be quite embarrassing and intrusive. Moreover, if family members disagree over who is to be appointed as the conservator or guardian, the proceedings may well become even more disagreeable and drawn out. The longevity of the proceedings can substantially increase the costs, especially as lawyers will need to be hired.

While the court will usually appoint a close family member to act as your conservator, it is under no obligation to do so. As such, it could end up appointing a stranger — someone who does not know you, who is not aware of your wishes, and who can legally ignore your family's requests and needs. For this reason alone, and forgetting the cost of such appointments, conservatorships are best avoided.

A conservator will generally need to:

- post a bond (a type of insurance policy) in case he or she steals or misuses your property.
- prepare (or hire a lawyer or accountant to prepare) detailed financial reports and periodically file them with the court.
- get court approval before carrying out certain transactions, such as selling real estate or making investments.

The cost of all these items adds up; making conservatorships an expensive process which ultimately needs to be paid from your estate. Appointing an agent under your power of attorney is, when done right, far more flexible, and cheaper than a conservatorship and therefore an often favored alternative.

What If You Do Not Think You Need a Power of Attorney?

You may think that if you are married, have placed the majority of your possessions in a living trust or hold most of your property as a joint tenant, then you don't need a durable power of attorney. That can certainly be true in some respects; but in each case there is still a strong argument to have a durable power of attorney.

Marriage and Registered Civil Partnerships

If you are married or in a registered civil partnership, your spouse or partner will have a significant degree of authority to deal with property you own together. For example, he or she will be able to access joint bank accounts to pay bills, or sell stocks or shares held in a joint brokerage account. However, there may be certain jointly owned property that they cannot deal with.

In many states, a spouse or civil partner cannot sell jointly owned real estate or automobiles without the written consent of the other. Of course, if the other spouse or partner is incapacitated and cannot give their consent, the sale cannot proceed. This could have important consequences if, for example, assets needed to be sold to pay on-going medical expenses or other important expenses such as a mortgage repayment. If you were the main bread winner in your house, and your income suddenly stopped coming in, assets may need to be sold to pay bills.

If, on the other hand, you held property in your own name only rather than in the joint names of you and your spouse or registered civil partner, he or she will have no legal authority to deal with that property. Unless, of course, they had a durable power of attorney or court order.

Living Trusts

Even if you have taken the time to create a living trust, and transferred most of your assets to the trust, it is still a good idea to have a durable power of attorney.

Under typical living trusts, the person appointed as the 'successor trustee' has the power to distribute the trust assets following the death of the 'grantor'. The grantor is the person who created the trust and transferred the assets into it. He or she normally manages the trust assets until no longer able to do so due to death or incapacity. In the case of incapacity, successor trustees have the power to step in and manage the trust assets on behalf of the trust's beneficiaries.

So, you may think you are covered if most of your assets are held in a living trust. If anything happens you, your successor trustee steps in and manages everything.

Of course, one of the most common problems with living trusts is that grantors often forget to transfer all their assets into the trust, or fail to correctly transfer them in. Suppose you bought investment assets about a month before you suffered a stroke….and you simply never got around to transferring those assets into your living trust. These types of issues happen all the time. Similarly, what if you signed transfer papers to transfer assets into the trust but, unknown to you, they were invalid for some reason. Again, this happens.

For these reasons, it is sensible to have a durable power of attorney just in case things don't' go to plan.

Resource

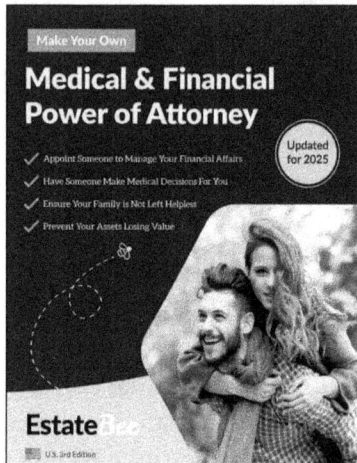

Make Your Own Medical & Financial Powers of Attorney

The importance of having powers of attorney is often underappreciated. They allow people you trust to manage your property and financial affairs during periods in which you are incapacitated; as well as make medical decisions on your behalf based on the instructions in your power of attorney document. This ensures that your affairs don't go unmanaged if you are incapacitated and you don't receive any unwanted medical treatments.

This book provides all the necessary documents and step-by-step instructions to make a power of attorney to cover virtually any situation.

Get your copy at www.estate-bee.com/product/make-your-own-medical-financial-powers-of-attorney

Joint Tenancy

Joint tenancy is a form of joint ownership where each co-owner holds an undivided interest in a piece of property. When one of the co-owners dies, the remaining co-owners automatically inherit the deceased co-owner's share of the property through a right of survivorship.

While matters are relatively straight-forward in the case of death, they can become more complicated where one of the co-owners becomes incapacitated. This is because the other co-owners will often have limited authority to deal with the joint tenancy property without the consent of the incapacitated co-owner.

Real estate provides a good example of this problem. If one co-owner becomes incapacitated, the others have no legal authority to sell or refinance the incapacitated co-owner's share of the property. In that case, they would be stuck holding the real estate on the same financing terms as were in place when the co-owner became incapacitated.

This type of problem could be avoided if the incapacitated co-owner had made a durable power of attorney. That durable power of attorney could authorize an agent to deal with the co-owner's share of joint tenancy property. That could include dealing with bank accounts, re-financings, and sales, as well as insurance and litigation matters. This would then give the remaining co-owners a means by which they could deal with the real estate. They would need the agent's consent of course, but that is something they would have to work on.

The Relationship Between Principal and Agent

One of the principal features underlying the relationship between a principal and an agent is the requirement that the agent acts with the utmost good faith on behalf of the principal. It is a relationship built on trust in which the agent is obliged to act with loyalty on behalf of the principal and in accordance with instructions received from the principal. The agent can neither intentionally ignore these instructions nor act negligently in the performance of them. In return for this loyalty, a principal instills confidence and trust in the agent thereby creating a fiduciary relationship of trust and confidence between the parties. It is this relationship of trust and confidence that underlies every specific action taken, or left untaken, by the agent.

Unfortunately, human nature being what it is, the principles of trust upon which the fiduciary relationship is built are often honored more on paper than in observance. The reality is that people sometimes succumb to the pressure of other affairs, to a lack of thought about and appreciation of their obligations, and of course to temptation. This risk of breach is the primary risk associated with agency relationships, particularly because of the agent's ability to bind the principal.

Who Can Be an Agent?

While there is no need for an agent to be a lawyer or other professional person, he or she must be an adult capable of making decisions and carrying out specific tasks on your behalf. What is more, if the power of attorney you intend to create is one for healthcare, it may be advisable to weigh the agent's capacity for compassion as more valuable than their talents as a financial analyst or businessman.

The agent cannot be an un-discharged bankrupt and should not be the owner, operator or employee of a nursing home or extended care facility in which the principal is resident. Neither can the agent be a witness to the principal's signature on the power of attorney.

Joint or Joint and Independent Agents

Sometimes a principal will want to appoint one or more agents to act on his/her behalf. Where the principal makes such a decision, he or she needs to decide whether the agents will be "joint" agents or "joint and independent" agents.

Joint agents must act together. As such, they must unanimously agree on a course of action before that action can proceed. Furthermore, joint agents must take the same action at the same time. For instance, if one of the agents is missing or unwilling to engage in a specific action, the remaining agents are powerless to act. This type of arrangement adds a degree of protection to the principal as it removes the possibility of any of the agents acting outside their instructions or in a "rogue" capacity. Joint and independent agents, on the other hand, can act either together or individually. As such, while both or all agents may be acting on behalf of the same principal and in relation to the same matter, they will not be obligated to consult with each other before taking an action which can bind the principal.

It is recommended that you avoid appointing joint agents. Rather, if more than one is to be appointed, it is preferable to appoint agents as alternates to the original agent.

Alternate Agents

While it is not necessary to do so, it is always a particularly good idea to appoint an alternate agent (also known as a substitute agent). The authority conferred on an alternate agent will only come into effect if the primary agent is unable or unwilling to act on behalf of the principal. In such circumstances, the alternate agent will acquire full power to act (unless expressly restricted) under the power of attorney.

In many cases, third parties (particularly financial institutions) will require proof that the original agent is unable or unwilling to act as agent under the power of attorney before accepting instructions from the alternate agent. In such cases, it's often useful for an alternate agent to request a signed confirmation from the principal revoking the authority of the original agent or, if available, from the original agent confirming in writing his or her refusal or inability to act as agent.

Scope of an Agent's Powers

Depending on whether the power of attorney is general or limited in nature, your agent will have as many or as few powers as the principal specifies in the power of attorney. Within the scope of the authority you confer on your agent, he or she can do anything that you can legally do.

You can give your agent authority to do some or all the following:

- Use your assets to discharge the day-to-day expenses of you and your family.
- Purchase, sell, lease, let, maintain, repair, pay taxes on and mortgage real estate and other property.
- Claim and collect social insurance, government, civil, military, and other entitlements.
- Invest money in stocks, bonds, and mutual funds.
- Effect transactions with financial institutions.
- Buy, maintain, and sell insurance policies and annuities.
- File and discharge your tax liabilities.
- Operate your small business.
- Claim real estate or other property that you inherit or are otherwise entitled to.
- Transfer property into a trust you have created (if the rules of the trust permit).
- Engage someone to represent you in court or to run legal actions on your behalf.
- Manage your affairs generally.

The above list is not exhaustive.

Duties and Responsibilities of an Agent

Your agent has the following primary duties and responsibilities:

- To act in your best interest.
- To keep accurate records of dealings and transactions undertaken on your behalf.
- To act towards you with the utmost good faith and to avoid situations where there is a conflict of interest.
- To keep your property and money separate from their own.

As far as keeping accurate records is concerned, the agent should keep a list or register of:

- All the principal's assets as of the date of his first transaction.
- All assets acquired and disposed of and the date and particulars of each such transaction.
- All receipts and disbursements and the date and particulars of each such transaction.
- All investments bought and sold and the date and particulars of each such transaction.
- All the principal's liabilities as of the date of the agent's first transaction.
- All liabilities incurred and paid and the date and particulars of each such transaction.
- All compensation taken by the agent and the way it was calculated.

Your agent should keep these records until he or she ceases acting for you and until the date upon which he or she is relieved from acting as your agent. These records should be handed over to the agent's successor, or if the power of attorney terminates by reason of the principal's death, to the principal's legal personal representative. Of course, if the principal has merely recovered from incapacity, the records can be given back to the principal directly.

Choosing an Agent

Your agent will be acting on your behalf, and as such the person you choose should obviously be someone you know and trust thoroughly. In making any decisions, you must bear in mind that your agent will have complete authority to deal with your financial and legal affairs (subject to any limitations or restrictions specified in your power of attorney).

You should ensure that the person you choose has adequate financial management skills and sufficient time to handle your affairs properly. Your agent must be available when required, be able to objectively make decisions, and be able to keep accurate financial records.

What Laws Govern My Power of Attorney?

A power of attorney is normally governed by the law specified in the document itself, or by the law of the jurisdiction in which the actions of the agent are to be performed. Normally, this is the place in which the property or assets of the principal are located. For this reason, it makes sense to appoint an agent located in that specific jurisdiction. If you anticipate that your agent will be acting in more than one jurisdiction, you should consider making separate powers of attorney for each jurisdiction.

A jurisdiction is essentially a place that has its own laws. Among others, this can be a county, a state, or a country.

If your power of attorney is to be used in a foreign country, you may have to have it "authenticated" or "legalized" before it can lawfully be used. This is a process whereby a government official certifies that the signature of the authority (usually a notary or lawyer) on your document is authentic and, as such, should be accepted in the foreign country. For more information about document authentication and legalization, contact the local consulate/embassy of the foreign country in which you propose your power of attorney to be used.

Most jurisdictions have their own power of attorney forms, but it is generally not mandatory that you use them. For example, lawyers frequently prepare powers of attorney for their clients using their standard terminology rather than adopting state approved forms. As long as the document is headed "power of attorney," specifies the parties, is signed and dated, and contains recognizable terms normally found in a power of attorney, it should be accepted by most authorities and organizations as such.

In addition to law firms, banks and brokerage houses often have their own power of attorney forms. If you want to ensure that your agent can transact business on your behalf with these institutions, you should consider preparing two (or more) powers of attorney — one being your own form and the others being those required by the institutions with which you propose to do business through your agent. You should obviously check with the relevant institutions in advance to ascertain their specific requirements, and even obtain copies of the forms they prefer to use. That way, you can fill in and sign their form at the same time as you prepare and execute your general-purpose power of attorney.

In terms of signing and witnessing, different jurisdictions tend to have different requirements for powers of attorney. These requirements can vary depending on the powers to be conferred on the agent and the type of power of attorney you are executing. As such, you will need to check the laws applicable in your state to see how your power of attorney should be executed. In most cases, however, executing your power of attorney in front of a witness or a notary will suffice.

Witness to a Power of Attorney

To satisfy various jurisdictional requirements, it is advisable that you not use one of the following people as your witnesses:

- Your spouse.
- Your partner.
- Your child.
- Your agent or alternate agent.
- The spouse of your agent or alternate agent.
- Employees of a medical facility in which you are a patient.

Your witnesses must be of legal age in your jurisdiction (see Chapter 2 above). They must also have legal capacity and be of sound mind.

Commencement of a Power of Attorney

A power of attorney will start on a date specified in the document or, in some cases, upon the occurrence of a specified event. If there is no specified date or event, a power of attorney starts immediately upon notification to the agent, following its execution by the principal and appropriate witnessing.

A durable power of attorney can be drafted to start at either the time of its signing, or upon the incapacity of the principal.

Revocation of a Power of Attorney

Provided you are not incapacitated, you can revoke a power of attorney at any time by sending a "notice of revocation of a power of attorney" to your agent. This is a written legal notice signed by or on behalf of a person who granted a power of attorney stating that he or she is terminating the powers conferred on the agent under an earlier power of attorney.

There are several reasons, practical and personal, why someone might want to revoke a power of attorney. For example, you might want to revoke a power of attorney because:

- The power of attorney is no longer necessary as you are now able to act on your own behalf.

- You no longer trust the agent who is acting on your behalf.

- You have found a more suitable person to act as your agent.

- It is no longer practical to have your agent acting on your behalf.

- The purpose behind originally granting the power of attorney has been fulfilled and you no longer need an agent to act on your behalf.

The revocation of a power of attorney is not effective against the agent or any third party who may rely on it until such time that notice of the revocation has been received by that party. As such, it is common practice to have a written notice evidencing the revocation rather than simply trying to revoke the authority orally. This written document can, in turn, be sent (by recorded delivery, if necessary) to all third parties who may rely on the power of attorney to put them on notice that your agent's authority has been revoked.

Important Points & Recommendation

While a power of attorney can be an exceptionally handy tool, it is important to remember that it is a serious legal document with far-reaching consequences. Therefore, drawing up and signing a power of attorney is something that you should not do without due care and forethought. And while you can pick up a power of attorney form online or at a business supply store and then fill it out yourself, you should be cautious about the forms you use. Indeed, you should only use forms from reputable vendors such as EstateBee. If you are in any doubt as to the adequacy of the forms or what they do, speak to a lawyer before using them.

CHAPTER 7 | # Advance Medical Directives

What Is an Advance Medical Directive?

An advance medical directive (or an "AMD" as it is also called) is a written statement in which you set out the medical care that you wish to receive during any period in which you are unable to make decisions on your own behalf. You can use AMDs to set out your preferences in relation to the receipt and non-receipt of various types of medical treatments and procedures including life sustaining procedures. These preferences will ordinarily be honored by medical personnel if you are admitted to a hospital or healthcare facility; assuming of course they have a copy of your directive.

Why Do I Need an Advance Medical Directive?

If the absence of having an AMD, state laws will generally allow your close family members to make medical decisions for you during any period in which you are incapacitated and unable to make decisions on your own behalf. While this can of course be beneficial for you, there is always a risk that your family members will make decisions based on what they believe is best for you rather than what you would have actually wanted in the circumstances. More importantly, there is the added risk that the person making these decisions for you might not be someone that you would have entrusted this responsibility to had you the choice. It was in anticipation of these very issues that AMDs were developed. Thankfully, all states now have provisions that allow for the use of AMDs so that people can exercise some control over the medical treatment they receive during periods of incapacity. The most common types of AMD currently in use include a living will and a durable power of attorney for healthcare. We will discuss each of these in turn below.

Living Wills and Their Background

A living will is a legal document that allows you to express your preferences regarding the receipt or non-receipt of certain life-prolonging medical procedures in the event that you become terminally ill or permanently unconscious and unable to communicate your own wishes. Apart from allowing you to specify your preferences in this respect, it also allows you to designate an agent who has authority to either enforce or revoke the terms of your AMD should the agent feel that the circumstances warrant.

The development of living wills can be viewed as a legal response to advancements made in the medical field over the last 100 years. During that period, both medicine and medical techniques advanced to a point where physicians can sustain life even in the direst of situations including situations that were once fatal. Physicians can treat diabetes, cancer and even organ failures. In many cases, patients can lead a relatively normal life following the treatment. However, in other cases, the quality of life of the patient is severely affected. In some instances, physicians can keep the body alive but are unable to restore movement or brain activity and the patient is left in a permanent vegetative state. The ability to keep a person alive in such a condition has invariably led to conflicts between the families of the patients and the physicians providing medical care to the patient. Notwithstanding that families may wish to have their loved ones die where there is no reasonable prospect of the patient surviving, medical practitioners will wish to exercise a moral and professional obligation to keep the patient alive. Given this clear conflict of interest, it may surprise you to learn that living wills have only been legal for a relatively short period.

In fact, the concept of facilitating a dying person's rights to control decisions about their own medical care was only first raised by attorney Luis Kutner in 1967 and taken up the following year by Florida legislator Dr. Walter Sackett. All initial attempts to pass bills to enable people to have this right failed. It was not until 1974, when State Senator Barry Keene presented similar bills in California, that things started to change. Although Senator Keene's initial attempts also failed, the bill was finally passed in 1976 with California becoming the first state to legally sanction a form of living will. Other states soon followed, and by the next year living will legislation had been introduced in 43 states and adopted in seven. Within 15 years all 50 states (plus the District of Columbia) passed some form of advance medical directive or living will legislation.

In 1990, the U.S. Supreme Court became involved when it agreed to hear its first case on the right to refuse or terminate life-sustaining treatment. The case in question was Cruzan vs. Director, Missouri Department of Health. On the night of January 11, 1983, Nancy Cruzan rolled her car and was found face down in bushes neither breathing nor with any detectable heartbeat. Paramedics restored both functions, but she remained unconscious. At the hospital, surgeons implanted a feeding and hydration tube, but all efforts at rehabilitation proved unavailing as Nancy, though able to breathe, fell deeper into a persistent vegetative state.

For six years Nancy Cruzan's physical and mental state grew steadily worse. It became clear that Nancy had no chance of regaining her faculties, and her parents asked the hospital to turn off her artificial nutrition and hydration processes. All agreed that this would cause her death, and the hospital declined to do so without court approval.

The Missouri Supreme Court, affirming a decision of the state court, ruled that a competent person had the constitutionally protected right to refuse medical treatment, even life sustaining treatment. However, it noted the same right did not apply to persons who were in a state of incompetence as they could not legally refuse the medical treatment. As a result, the focus in the Cruzan case changed to considering whether a surrogate could make such a decision on Nancy's behalf.

Missouri had designed its legislation to include surrogates, subject to the procedural safeguard that there was "clear and convincing evidence" that the patient while competent had expressed the desire not to be kept alive in a permanently vegetative state. On appeal, the U.S. Supreme Court recognized a patient's right to refuse life-sustaining treatment through the use of a written document that complies with applicable state law, and found that Missouri's safeguard was both permissible and constitutional where evidence of intention had been documented. However, it ruled that this standard of proof had not been satisfied in the Cruzan case. In reaching this conclusion, the court affirmed the state court's decision against the petitioning parents, which had held that they had not proven the case that Nancy had expressed a strong desire that her life never be artificially maintained.

Fortunately, the Cruzan family did not stop, and were finally able to muster enough proof of Nancy's desire not to be artificially kept alive. They eventually won a court order to discontinue her life support, and she finally died 11 days later on December 26, 1990.

Congress has now passed legislation to publicize and support the state laws. These laws go under the name Advance Medical Directives and, rather than creating any new forms of directives, they simply validate state laws that create AMDs. The AMD laws derive from the federal Patient Self-Determination Act, 1991 ("PSDA"), passed a short while after the Cruzan decision. The PSDA requires that adult patients admitted to medical care facilities in receipt of federal funding be apprised of their rights to prepare advance healthcare directives which, if prepared, are then entered on their medical records.

How Living Wills Work

In understanding how living wills work in practice, it is important that you realize that living wills only come into effect when:

- you are suffering from a terminal condition or a persistent comatose condition or are in a permanent vegetative state;
- there is no real prospect of your recovery; and
- you are unable to make and communicate your own healthcare decisions.

Only at this point will the person nominated under your living will have any ability to enforce or revoke any of the instructions that you have set out in your living will. However, the law in the majority of states (and indeed the terms of most living wills) requires that before your nominated person can lawfully act, two physicians must first personally examine you and agree that you satisfy the conditions referred to above and that the application of medical procedures would only prolong the dying process. If both doctors agree that this is the case, then the medical procedures may be withdrawn or applied, depending on the choices expressed in your living will.

What Is a Terminal Condition?

A terminal condition is an incurable condition caused by disease, illness, or injury with the consequence that there is no reasonable prospect that the patient's condition will improve, and the expected result is death. Such diagnoses are often common with progressive diseases such as cancer or advanced heart disease.

Did You Know ?

A terminal condition is referred to in some states as a terminal illness, a terminal injury or an incurable or irreversible illness.

Usually, a patient is considered terminally ill when the life expectancy is estimated to be six months or less under the assumption that the disease will run its normal course. In many cases, where people are correctly diagnosed as being terminally ill, they will cease to be able to effectively communicate towards the final stages of their illness. It is in these very situations that living wills can be most beneficial.

What Is a Persistent Comatose Condition?

A persistent comatose condition can generally be described as a profound or deep state of unconsciousness where there is no reasonable prospect of regaining consciousness. In other words, while we are in fact alive, we are effectively asleep and unable to respond to life around us. This condition, which is often caused by accidents or traumas, is like a coma save that with a coma there is often an expectation that the patient will regain consciousness at some time in the future.

What Is a Persistent Vegetative Condition?

A persistent vegetative state, which sometimes follows a coma, is a condition which results in a person losing all cognitive neurological function and awareness of the environment around them. However, despite this neurological illness, the individual retains non-cognitive functions and a disrupted sleep-wake cycle.

What Life Support Choices Do I Have Within My Living Will?

There are three principal choices you can make in respect of life-sustaining measures:

Option 1—You can require doctors do everything in their power to keep you alive.

Option 2—You can provide that the only life-sustaining measures you desire to have are artificial tube feeding for nutrition (food) and hydration (water).

Option 3 — You can have all artificial life-sustaining treatment withheld, including nutrition and hydration.

Of course, you can to a degree mix some of the above options. However, no matter which of these three options you choose, you will generally always be provided with all necessary pain medication and comfort medication. In addition to the provision of treatment for pain and comfort, there are a number of different treatments available to help keep you alive including surgery, respiratory support, dialysis, antibiotics, cardiac resuscitation, blood transfusions, tissue and organ donation, and receipt of nutrition and hydration.

Should I Make a Living Will?

Whether or not you decide to make a living will is completely up to you. In making that decision, you will need to consider situations that might leave you in a persistent state of unconsciousness or indeed cause your death. Understandably, these are situations you might prefer not to think about. However, with high-tech medicine adding weeks, months and sometimes years to our lives (rather than adding "life" to our years), we all run the risk of being incapacitated before we die. This leaves some serious questions for you, and indeed everyone, to ponder and to plan for.

Consider what you would want to happen if a serious accident or illness left you in a situation where:

- You are unable to speak, move, feel or are in constant pain.
- Only a respirator and feeding tube are keeping you alive.
- Your quality of life is virtually non-existent and there is no real hope of improvement.

Would you want to stretch your life out on life support, or would you rather let nature take its course? Where would you want to draw the line? When should it end?

Unfortunately, far too many people find themselves in those or similar situations without warning and without the benefit of having asked and answered those questions. These people have no control over the medical care they are receiving. These people have no choice but to "live." You can avoid this if you are practical. Consider your alternatives and make a choice.

If this choice is hard for you to contemplate, think of how it will be for your loved ones if you do nothing. If anything should ever happen to you, they will be the ones who will have to bear the emotional trauma of dealing with your permanent incapacity. They will be the ones that will have to visit you in a hospital and make the tough decisions for you. They will be the ones who must consider how to foot the bill for years of hospital care notwithstanding that there might be no possible chance of recovery for you. They may even end up paying these bills themselves.

We do not mean in this chapter to scare you, or to convince you whether it is right or wrong to make a living will. Our goal is just to prompt you into thinking about this important matter for yourself. The decision about whether to make a living will is, of course, yours to make.

But having the right to decide what medical treatment you receive, if any, during a terminal illness is what living wills are all about. They allow you to decide these things now, while you can. It is about doing it calmly and without any pressure, and then articulating your wishes in a legal document that will be there to guide your doctors, friends and family if and when you come into the emergency room unable to tell them what you really want.

Important Note

A living will does not allow you to appoint another to make life-sustaining decisions for you; that power can only be granted under a power of attorney. Your agent under a living will typically only has powers of enforcement or revocation.

State Requirements for Life Sustaining Medical Treatment

Although you may have a living will, certain states have legal restrictions and requirements concerning medical treatment that must be adhered to notwithstanding the terms of your living will. For example, some states require that you receive medical treatment for a certain period regardless of your living will. In these states, if you are diagnosed to be in a state of permanent unconsciousness, laws may require that you receive medical treatment for 60 or 90 days before the doctors can make a decision to implement your wishes as stated in your living will. Or if your condition shows zero brain activity, laws may require that you receive medical treatment for a certain number of hours before the terms of your living will can be implemented.

Other legal limitations may also arise. For instance, the provisions in your state may prevent a living will from being implemented if a woman is pregnant and may declare that the living will is ineffective during the pregnancy.

To be certain of the effectiveness and legality of your living will, and learn what provisos state law may apply, it is best to contact a lawyer in your particular state - or ask a relevant government agency for information. To give you a flavor of some of the restrictions that apply, we have set out a summary of same below.

State	Overview of State Requirements for AMDs
Alabama	Two witnesses required for an AMD. An AMD will not be valid if the patient is pregnant.
Alaska	No witnesses required for a living will. Two witnesses are required for a healthcare power of attorney.
Arizona	A witness and a notary are required for both a living will and a healthcare power of attorney.
Arkansas	Two witnesses required for both a living will and a healthcare power of attorney. Neither will be valid if the patient is pregnant.
California	Two witnesses required for both an AMD and a healthcare power of attorney. A healthcare power of attorney can also be witnessed by a notary.
Colorado	Two witnesses required for an AMD. A healthcare power of attorney does not require any witnesses.
Connecticut	Two witnesses required for both an AMD and a healthcare power of attorney. The signatures must be notarized. Neither will be valid if the patient is pregnant.
Delaware, District of Columbia, Florida	Two witnesses required for both a living will and a healthcare power of attorney.
Georgia	Two witnesses required for both a living will and a healthcare power of attorney. A living will is not valid if the patient is pregnant.

Hawaii	Two witnesses required for both a living will and a healthcare power of attorney. The healthcare power of attorney must be notarized. A living will is not valid if the patient is pregnant.
Idaho	Two witnesses required for both a living will and a healthcare power of attorney. A notary can also witness a healthcare power of attorney. A living will is not valid if the patient is pregnant.
Illinois, Indiana	Two witnesses required for a living will. A living will is not valid if the patient is pregnant. One witness required for a healthcare power of attorney.
Iowa	Two witnesses and a notary required for both a living will and a healthcare power of attorney. A living will is not valid if the patient is pregnant.
Kansas	Two witnesses or a notary are required for a living will.
Kentucky	Two witnesses or a notary required for a living will. A living will is not valid if the patient is pregnant.
Louisiana, Maine, Maryland	Two witnesses required for both a living will and a healthcare power of attorney.
Massachusetts	No provision for a format of living will. Two witnesses required for both a living will and a healthcare power of attorney.
Michigan	No provision for a format of living will. Two witnesses required for both a living will and a healthcare power of attorney.
Minnesota	Two witnesses and a notary required for both a living will and a healthcare power of attorney. A living will is not valid if the patient is pregnant.
Mississippi	Two witnesses required for an advanced healthcare directive (includes both a living will and a healthcare power of attorney in the one document).

Missouri	Two witnesses required for both a living will and a healthcare power of attorney. A notary can also witness a healthcare power of attorney. A living will is not valid if the patient is pregnant.
Montana	Two witnesses required for a living will.
Nebraska	Two witnesses and a notary required to witness a living will.
Nevada	Two witnesses required for both a living will and a healthcare power of attorney. A notary can also witness a healthcare power of attorney.
New Hampshire	Two witnesses or a notary required to witness both a living will and a healthcare power of attorney.
New Jersey	Two witnesses or a notary or a lawyer is required to witness both living wills and healthcare powers of attorney.
New Mexico, New York	No witnesses required for either a living will or a healthcare power of attorney.
North Carolina	Two witnesses required for both a living will and a healthcare power of attorney. A living will is not valid if the patient is pregnant.
North Dakota	Two witnesses required for both a living will and a healthcare power of attorney. A living will is not valid if the patient is pregnant.
Ohio	Two witnesses or a notary required for both a living will and a healthcare power of attorney. A living will is generally not valid if the patient is pregnant.
Oklahoma	Two witnesses required for both a living will and a healthcare power of attorney. A living will is not valid if the patient is pregnant.
Oregon	Two witnesses required for both a living will and a healthcare power of attorney.

Pennsylvania	Two witnesses required for a living will (includes a healthcare power of attorney in the same document). A living will is not valid if the patient is pregnant.
Rhode Island	Two witnesses or a notary required for both a living will and a healthcare power of attorney. A living will is generally not valid if the patient is pregnant.
South Carolina	Two witnesses or a notary required for both a living will and a healthcare power of attorney. A living will also requires a notary to act as a witness.
South Dakota	Two witnesses required for both a living will and a healthcare power of attorney. A healthcare power of attorney can also be witnessed by a notary. A living will is generally not valid if the patient is pregnant.
Tennessee	Two witnesses required for both a living will and a healthcare power of attorney. A healthcare power of attorney can also be witnessed by a notary.
Texas	Two witnesses required for both a living will and a healthcare power of attorney. A living will is generally not valid if the patient is pregnant.
Utah	Two witnesses required for a living will. A living will is generally not valid if the patient is pregnant. A notary is required for a healthcare power of attorney.
Vermont	Two witnesses required for both a living will and a healthcare power of attorney.
Virginia	An advance medical directive requires two witnesses.
Washington	Two witnesses required for a living will. A living will is generally not valid if the patient is pregnant. No witnesses are required for a healthcare power of attorney.
West Virginia	Two witnesses and a notary required for both a living will and a healthcare power of attorney.

Wisconsin	Two witnesses and a notary required for both a living will and a healthcare power of attorney. A living will is not valid if the patient is pregnant.
Wyoming	Two witnesses are required for both a living will and a healthcare power of attorney. A notary is also required for a healthcare power of attorney. A living will is not valid if the patient is pregnant.

Witness Requirements

In order to ensure that a living will is the voluntary act of the person making it, and that this person has not been unduly influenced by their medical condition or by other persons, certain states have limitations on when a living will can be made and who can act as a witnesses to its execution.

In several states, you cannot make a living will while you are in the hospital or in a nursing home. It must be made before you go to the hospital (or after you have been discharged and before you are readmitted with your "final illness"). In other states, specific conditions will apply before you can make a living will in a hospital. Under Georgia law, for example, if you wish to make a living will while you are a patient in a hospital or resident in a nursing home, you will need to have an additional person witness you signing your living will form. In the case of a hospital, this third witness must be the chief of the hospital staff or a physician not participating in your care. In the case of a nursing home, it must be the nursing home's medical director or a staff physician not participating in your care.

In most cases, you will need two people to witness the signing of your living will. However, several states prohibit certain people from acting as a witness. You should check the laws of your state in this respect. In general, however, the following people are precluded from acting as witnesses in most states: your spouse, children, grandchildren, parents, grandparents, siblings, any lineal ancestors, or descendants, and any of these persons' spouses. Other people who should not be witnesses include someone who is named in your last will or who would benefit from your estate (if you died intestate), someone who is a beneficiary of a life insurance policy on your life, or a person who is directly responsible for your medical care (including employees, agents and patients of any hospital or nursing home that you might be in). The rationale here is that each of those people may potentially gain upon your death and may make decisions based on self-motivation. You should also avoid using minors as witnesses.

Appointing an Agent to Revoke or Enforce Your Living Will

As previously mentioned, some states allow you to name an agent who may either revoke or enforce your living will. It is generally considered that when you name an agent, you are giving that person the power and authority to go to court on your behalf and ask a judge to either revoke or enforce the terms of your living will. However, in some cases, depending on the content of your living will, the agent does not need to go to court, but can merely instruct the medical care providers to either disregard or to enforce your wishes as set out in the living will. Alternatively, the agent may only be able to temporarily suspend the operation of your living will so that it is not used at a specific time but may be used later.

Important Note

Even if you do not appoint an agent under your living will, healthcare facilities and physicians are still obliged to follow the provisions set out in your living will.

Appointing a person to enforce or revoke your healthcare decisions can be useful because it allows for advocacy on your behalf which could help get over difficulties in interpreting your living will. It is also worth remembering that if a physician refuses to respect the terms of your living will you have the right to be transferred to another physician or hospital that will honor your wishes. An agent can be useful in ensuring that this happens.

Finalizing Your Living Will

Once you have decided to make a living will, you should check the specific laws that may apply in your state. Many states have specific forms, and a few states have required language that should be included in your living will. When you have determined the specific laws that apply in your state and what form you need to use, there are a few final steps you should take to ensure that your wishes will be respected when the time comes. Specifically, you should:

- Discuss the terms of your advance directive with your doctor before you sign it. Make sure you are both comfortable with what it says. He or she may suggest something you had not thought of that you might decide to include.

- Comply with your state's signature and witness requirements. As mentioned above, states have various requirements about who can be a witness, how many witnesses are needed, and if the directive must be notarized.

- Provide copies of the signed directive to (1) your doctor and hospital; (2) your agent, if one is named; (3) family members; (4) your lawyer; and (5) other significant people in your life.

Important Note

Out-of-State Directives

People often wonder whether advance directives made in one state will be honored in other states. The good news is that the laws of many states provide for the recognition of living wills made in other states. However, there are some states where the law is simply not clear on the issue. While there is a degree of ambiguity in these states, the practical reality is that most healthcare providers will try to abide by your wishes irrespective of whether you use an out-of-state form or not.

In situations where you spend much of your time between a few different states, it might be useful to make a living will in each state just to cover the possibility that a healthcare provider refuses to recognize an out-of-state living will. It might even be practical to have different healthcare agents in each such state, but this is something that you will have to consider carefully.

Terminating Advance Directives

If you remain mentally competent and able to manage your own affairs, you may terminate a living will that you have previously made at any time. Incidentally, the same applies to a healthcare power of attorney.

While your advance directive can be revoked orally, even as in some cases it can be made orally, we do not recommend doing so. It is simply too prone to challenge, and too difficult to prove. Rather, we would recommend one of the following options:

- physically destroying the living will by burning, tearing, or shredding it;
- revoking the authority granted to an agent under a living will by giving notice of revocation in writing; or
- if you have appointed a proxy or attorney-in-fact with power to do so, this person can revoke your directive.

Ordinarily, revocation only takes effect when the revocation is communicated to the agent or the person who may rely on the living will. So, if you revoke your living will, we recommend that you should send copies of the notice of revocation to each person or facility that holds a copy of your living will. This should ensure that the notice is brought to their attention.

Not all states require that your revocation be signed in front of witnesses, but a handful of states do. Even if your state does not require witnesses, it is a good idea to have them sign your revocation. With witnesses, you minimize the chances that your revocation will be challenged or considered ineffective.

Family Discussions

Ordinarily, if you become incapacitated it will be up to your family to decide whether or not they wish to support the end-of-life decisions that you have made in your living will, or whether they will try and fight it with a view to keeping you alive or allowing you to die naturally. It is for this very reason that we recommend that you discuss your personal choices with close family members. At the very least, it will afford you an opportunity to bring them around to your way of thinking. Alternatively, it will open the door for a discussion that may provide you with useful feedback or may even present you with alternatives that you had not considered.

In having this discussion, you should explain to your family members the decisions you have made and why you have made them. It may even be useful to refer to some of the high-profile cases in this area such as the Cruzan case mentioned above, or the more recent and substantively similar Terri Schiavo case. It is important that you also try and get them to accept the person you have nominated as your agent under your living will. Otherwise, in addition to the emotional trauma, your family could find themselves amidst a grave conflict should you become incapacitated. It follows that it is also very important that you discuss your wishes with your agent and ensure that he or she is fully aware of what you want to happen should you ever become permanently incapacitated. If you get both your family and agent in line with your thinking on the subject, matters should hopefully run smoothly between them when the time requires that important decisions be made.

Making Your Wishes Known

When you have made your advance medical directive, it is a good idea to carry a card in your wallet or purse confirming that you have done so. This way, should you be admitted to a medical facility and unable to communicate, healthcare providers will be alerted to the fact that you have set out your requirements in relation to end-of-life treatments and will be legally bound to honor your wishes. By including on your card the contact names and numbers of key family members, details of your doctor, and details of the location of your advance directives if you have any, your healthcare providers will be able to determine your healthcare wishes when most needed.

Healthcare Power of Attorney

As you will have no doubt gathered from the foregoing, the principal limitation of living wills is that they only come into play when you are either terminally ill or permanently unconscious and cannot tell your doctors what you want done. It therefore does not apply where, for example, you are unconscious due to a minor accident or illness or where you are suffering from a mental illness. This is where a healthcare power of attorney comes into play.

A healthcare power of attorney (sometimes called a "durable power of attorney for healthcare" or a "healthcare proxy") is a document that appoints someone of your choice to be your authorized agent (or attorney-in-fact or proxy) for the purpose of making healthcare decisions on your behalf when you are unable to do so yourself. You can give your agent as much or as little authority as you wish to make some or all healthcare decisions for you. And in most states, you can include the same kind of instructions that you would put in a living will and require that your agent abides by them in carrying out his duties.

The authority is effective only when your attending physician or physicians (depending on state law and the terms of your healthcare power of attorney) determines that you have lost the capacity to make informed healthcare decisions for yourself. If you still have this capacity, you retain the right to make all medical and other healthcare decisions.

In your healthcare power of attorney, you may also limit the healthcare decisions that your agent will have the authority to make. The authority of the agent to make healthcare decisions for you generally will include the authority to:

- Give informed consent.
- Refuse to give informed consent.
- Withdraw informed consent.
- Arrange for the provision of any care, treatment, service, or procedure designed to maintain, diagnose, or treat a physical or mental condition.

Choosing a Healthcare Agent

The person you choose to be your healthcare agent (also called an "attorney-in-fact" or "proxy for healthcare decisions") should be a trusted individual who is also knowledgeable and comfortable discussing healthcare issues. Because this person may need to argue your case with doctors or family members, or even go to court, an assertive yet diplomatic individual may be the best person to represent your interests. Your representative should be aware of the choices you have made in your advance directives and should support those instructions.

For most, the person chosen to act as an agent is a spouse, partner, or close family relative. However, despite the fact that you trust these people, you still need to consider whether they have the resolve to make the tough decisions that you have asked them to make when the time comes. If you are in any doubt, you may wish to choose an alternative agent or appoint a second agent who independently has full authority to carry out your instructions. However, we would not ordinarily recommend the appointment of joint agents as it can lead to arguments and conflicts between them which result in delays in important medical decisions being made.

In choosing an agent, you should consider the person's age, emotional ability, how well they know you, their views on your wishes and the right to life generally, their religious beliefs, whether they have any financial or other interest in your survival or death, and the availability of that person generally to act as your agent.

Conclusion

You now have two important ways to prepare for the possibility that, someday, you may be unable to decide for yourself what medical treatments to accept or refuse. We recommend that you consider the use of a living will and a healthcare power of attorney carefully as they form an integral part of estate planning.

Resource

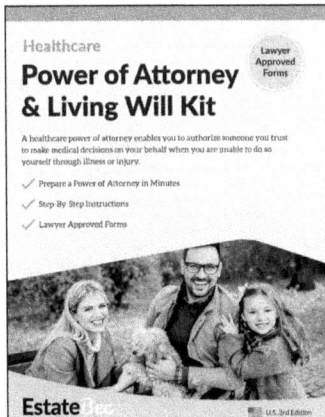

Healthcare
Power of Attorney & Living Will Kit

Lawyer Approved Forms

A healthcare power of attorney enables you to authorize someone you trust to make medical decisions on your behalf when you are unable to do so yourself through illness or injury.

✓ Prepare a Power of Attorney in Minutes
✓ Step-By-Step Instructions
✓ Lawyer Approved Forms

Estate Bee   U.S. 3rd Edition

Healthcare Power of Attorney & Living Will Kit

This Healthcare Power of Attorney & Living Will Kit allows you to appoint an agent to make medical decisions on your behalf if you are unconscious or otherwise unable to do so yourself. It also allows you to set out your preferences regarding the receipt or non-receipt of life sustaining medical treatments during any period in which you are permanently unconscious or suffering from a terminal illness and unable to communicate your wishes.

Your document only become effective if doctors determine that you don't have the capacity to make your own healthcare decisions.

This Kit contains all the information and ready-to-use lawyer prepared legal forms and documents necessary to create a combined Healthcare Power of Attorney and Living Will.

Get your copy at www.estate-bee.com/product/helathcare-power-of-attorney-living-will-kit/

CHAPTER 8

Probate Avoidance Measures

Probate Avoidance

As discussed in Chapter 5, probate is a court supervised administrative process by which the assets of a deceased person are gathered, applied to pay debts, taxes, and expenses of administration, and then distributed to the beneficiaries named in the deceased's last will and testament. Where there is no will, the assets go through a similar process known as intestate administration. For ease, we will refer only to the probate process in this chapter.

While some states have procedures to allow for a speedy probate process for "small estates," the average probate takes at least six months to complete. If there are any difficulties in locating beneficiaries or assets, or if there are legal challenges to the validity of the deceased's will, this time frame can increase dramatically, and probate can take several years to complete. Only when the process is completed in full should the executor transfer the remainder of the deceased's estate to the relevant beneficiaries.

The probate process can be expensive—particularly if it drags on. The cost of probate differs from state to state and is generally determined by either state law or custom and practice in a particular area. When all the costs associated with probate are added up, the resulting cost is often between 1-7 percent (or even more) of the value of the deceased's probate estate. As some of these probate costs are set by state law there is little that you can do to mitigate or reduce them once in probate. However, in this chapter we discuss certain measures that will allow you to avoid probate, and the costs involved, with respect to some or all your assets.

There are several legal mechanisms which you can use to avoid probate, including:

- Pay-on-death, transfer-on-death, or joint accounts.
- Transfer-on-death securities.
- Insurance policies.
- Joint ownership of property.
- Revocable living trusts.
- Lifetime gifts.
- Taking advantage of a simplified procedure that many states allow for small estates.

These methods have several advantages. For example, they are flexible and easy to set up. Bank accounts and insurance policies can be established, amended, and terminated with little hassle or cost. As a result, you can easily and quickly change the beneficiaries of your assets or the amount by which you intend them to benefit by means of a simple visit to your local bank or insurance broker. And after you die, the only document that your beneficiaries will typically need to present to the bank or insurance company to receive the proceeds of their inheritance is a death certificate evidencing your death. With that, the financial institution should be happy to arrange to have the relevant proceeds transferred to your beneficiary's name or paid out to them.

There are also, however, disadvantages to using these methods. You need to be careful to ensure that all your probate alternatives are working together to avoid probate and, more importantly, to distribute your assets in accordance with the overall objectives of your estate plan. You will need to pay specific attention to the beneficiaries named on joint bank accounts and insurance policies, the way real estate is held. Any lack of attention could result in one person receiving a lot more than you had intended to the detriment of someone else. And keep in mind that by the time the problem materializes you may not be around to remedy it.

'Pay-on-Death' or 'Transfer-on-Death' Accounts

One of easiest ways to avoid probate is by having a "pay-on-death" (**POD**) or "transfer-on-death" (**TOD**) account. Most states now have laws that allow account holders to designate a named beneficiary who will receive the proceeds of their bank and/or investment accounts after they have died. When the account holder dies, the money in the designated account goes directly to the named beneficiary without going through probate.

Generally, there is no need to open a new account to avail of the advantages of a pay-on-death account. In many cases, you can add a "POD designation" to an existing account by simply adding the name or names of the beneficiaries to that account. The relevant financial institution will be able to give you information on what exactly needs to be done to add the designation.

During the account holder's lifetime, the designated beneficiaries have no rights whatsoever in relation to the account or its proceeds; and the account holder can close the account or remove the POD designation at any time. It is only after the death of the account holder that the beneficiaries become entitled to the proceeds.

TOD accounts are like POD accounts but are more commonly used to transfer ownership of stocks, bonds, and mutual funds.

'Transfer-on-Death' Securities

The "Transfer on Death Security Registration Act" provides for the transfer-on-death of stocks, shares, bonds and other financial instruments and securities. Like the TOD and POD accounts referred to above, these securities can be transferred on death to named beneficiaries free of the requirement to pass through probate.

To date, the following states have adopted the legislation (with modification in some instances): Alabama, Alaska, Arizona, Arkansas, California, Colorado, Connecticut, Delaware, District of Columbia, Florida, Georgia, Hawaii, Idaho, Illinois, Indiana, Iowa, Kansas, Kentucky, Maine, Maryland, Massachusetts, Michigan, Minnesota, Mississippi, Missouri, Montana, Nebraska, Nevada, New Hampshire, New Jersey, New Mexico, New York, North Carolina, North Dakota, Ohio, Oklahoma, Oregon, Pennsylvania, Rhode Island, South Carolina, South Dakota, Tennessee, Utah, and Vermont.

Only Louisiana and Texas have not adopted the legislation.

Retirement Accounts

Like POD accounts, it is also possible to designate beneficiaries of retirement accounts such as IRAs and 401(k)s. Your broker or financial advisor should be able to assist with the designation should you so wish.

Remember that you need to designate the beneficiary on the account documents; not in a will, living trust or elsewhere. If you do not comply with the relevant requirements, the proceeds may well end up going through probate.

Joint Accounts

Another easy way to avoid probate is by having joint accounts. Where an account is held in the name of two or more persons and is designated with the right of survivorship, then when one of the account holders dies, the surviving account holders will automatically acquire the deceased account holder's interest in the account. Whoever is the last surviving joint owner will ultimately own the proceeds of the account outright.

Where a transfer occurs on survivorship, there is no need for probate. The surviving account holder(s) will simply need to provide a copy of the deceased account holder's death certificate to the bank and the bank can then remove that person's name from the account.

Custodial Accounts

People often decide to set aside funds in the form of bank accounts, certificates of deposit, or similar securities as a nest egg for their minor children, grandchildren, or others to cover things like college expenses or simply to give them a start in life. One of the most common ways of doing this is by means of a custodial account.

A custodial account is like a trust in many ways but is not actually a trust. With a custodial account, the proceeds or assets (where the account is an investment account) are placed under the control of a person known as a custodian. The custodian will have no beneficial interest in the account and will simply manage the account on behalf of the minor beneficiary until he or she reaches a specified age.

It is important to note that once the custodial account is set up and the beneficiary named, the proceeds of the account then beneficially belong to the beneficiary. As such, you cannot take it back. Moreover, if the account generates any income, then that income also typically belongs to the beneficiary (there are some exceptions to this where the account is used to avoid tax) and tax returns may need to be made. The account will automatically terminate when the beneficiary reaches a specified age. Almost all states have a maximum prescribed age under either the Uniform Gifts to Minors Act (UGMA) 1956 or the Uniform Transfers to Minors Act (UTMA) 1986. For details of the age applicable in your state, see Chapter 2.

Turning back to probate, custodial accounts will not form part of your probate estate because the gift is deemed to have been made when the account was set up, not when you die or when the custodial account terminates.

Savings Bonds

Saving bonds, like bank accounts, can be held jointly and, like POD accounts, can contain a pay-on-death designation. In the case of jointly held savings bonds, these will pass to the survivor(s) on the death of the other bond holder(s). Also, where there is a POD designation, the bonds will pass to the named beneficiary on your death. In each case, probate will not be needed.

If the bonds are not held jointly or there is no POD designation, the bonds can only be redeemed by the executor. However, they may be reissued to the beneficiary under a will upon a request from the executor accompanied by a copy of the death certificate and the executor's grant of representation. Of course, this will be done as part of the probate process.

Life Insurance Proceeds

A life insurance policy is another example of a simple means by which you can avoid probate. Where you designate a named beneficiary under your life insurance policy, the proceeds of the policy which are payable on your death will pass directly to the named beneficiary without the need to go through probate. However, if your estate is named as the main beneficiary (which is unusual), or if no beneficiaries have been named, or if the named beneficiaries have died, the proceeds will need to pass through probate.

The insurance proceeds payable on your death are part of your estate for federal estate tax purposes and are ordinarily taxable. However, this can be avoided by transferring ownership of the policy to another person while you are still alive.

Joint Ownership of Property

Whether or not the property that you own at the time of your death will need to be probated depends on how the title to that property is held. Typically, property can be held in three different ways:

● Joint tenancy (survivorship).

- Tenancy by the entireties.
- Tenancy in common.

Joint Tenancy

We have already touched on the concept of joint tenancy in relation to bank accounts. The same principle applies to real estate. Where a property is held under a joint tenancy, each of the property owners has an undivided percentage interest in the entire property.

To illustrate joint tenancy, take a case where four people own a property equally under a joint tenancy arrangement. Each of the four owners has an entitlement to a 25 percent interest in the whole of the property. However, because each owner has an entitlement to a percentage of the whole, rather than having a divided and defined 25 percent interest in the property, he or she is entitled to access and take actions in respect of the entire property and not simply 25 percent of it.

When one joint tenant dies, his or her share passes to the remaining joint tenants. So, in our example, where one of the four property owners die, his or her share automatically passes to each of the three survivors, who then own an approximate 33.33% (or 1/3) interest in the property.

The key point for estate planning purposes is that the share passes from the deceased joint owner to the remaining joint owners without the need for probate. It follows that probate costs can be reduced or even eliminated by converting solely owned assets into jointly owned assets held under a joint tenancy.

Tenancy by the Entirety

A special type of joint tenancy, known as a "tenancy by the entirety," is recognized between married couples in some states. Under this form of joint ownership, if a married couple owns property as tenants by the entirety, then each spouse must obtain the consent of the other before dealing with the property in any way that would affect the rights of the other. This includes putting in place a mortgage over the property. Each spouse lacks the power to freely dispose of their interest under their will, or in any other way, as the principle of survivorship applies between the spouses.

Important Note

States that recognize a tenancy by the entirety include: Alaska*, Arkansas, Delaware, District of Columbia, Florida, Hawaii, Illinois*, Indiana*, Kentucky*, Maryland, Massachusetts, Michigan*, Mississippi, Missouri, New Jersey, New York*, North Carolina*, Ohio, Oklahoma, Oregon, Pennsylvania, Rhode Island, Tennessee, Utah, Vermont, Virginia and Wyoming.

*States that allow tenancy by entirety for real estate only

Tenancy in Common

A tenancy in common is one of the most common forms of property ownership in most states. A tenancy in common is created where two or more people purchase a property together as "tenants in common." As tenants in common, each of the parties own a separate and distinguishable part of the property. To take the example of our four property owners above, if the arrangement was a tenancy in common, each of them would own 25 percent of the property in their own right and would be free to sell that 25 per cent to any person at any time and/or to dispose of their interest under their will. The right of survivorship does not apply here.

Community Property

Community property states have different rules governing probate, so it is important to understand your own state's rules when planning the distribution of your estate on your death.

At the date of writing there are nine community property states namely Arizona, California, Idaho, Louisiana, Nevada, New Mexico, Texas, Washington, and Wisconsin. In Alaska couples can opt to have their property treated as community property under the terms of a written property agreement. Each of the above states has special laws that dictate how married people can own and dispose of their property—both real and personal.

Important Note

Real property is property such as land, buildings, and real estate generally. Personal property can be broadly defined as all other property which a person can own.

In a community property state, the law broadly provides that all earnings generated during a marriage and all property purchased during the marriage is considered "community property" and is therefore equally owned by each spouse. For example, if one spouse earns $100,000 per year as an executive, while the other earns $40,000 as a freelance writer, then each spouse shall be deemed to "own" $70,000 of those earnings. In addition to salary, property purchased by one spouse in his or her own name with money he or she earned during the marriage will also be regarded as community property. Similarly, debts incurred by either spouse during their marriage are regarded as debts of the couple rather than individual debts.

"Separate property," on the other hand, includes property received by a spouse during their marriage by means of a gift or bequest under a will. It also includes any property owned by a spouse before they got married which that spouse has kept segregated from community property during the marriage. Like the position regarding debts above, all debts incurred by spouses prior to marriage are considered separate debts of each spouse.

Separate property can also include anything that one spouse gives up in favor of the other spouse in writing.

The distinction between community property and separate property becomes important when determining which of a spouse's assets can be freely disposed of under the terms of their will. In community property states, on the death of a spouse, half of the community property owned by the couple will go to the surviving spouse unless the deceased spouse's will directs otherwise (i.e. provides for the transfer of part or all of their share of the community property to the surviving spouse). Otherwise, the surviving spouse is free to dispose of their share of community property as well as their separate property as they desire.

Revocable Living Trust

An additional way to avoid probate is to establish and fund a revocable living trust. This type of trust is established by writing a trust agreement under which the creator of the trust (known as the grantor) will transfer ownership of certain of his assets into the trust. The trustee of the trust (who is also the grantor) will hold title to and manage the assets on behalf of the trust. The trustee can manage, invest, and spend the trust property as he or she sees fit for the benefit of the grantor and for the benefit of the ultimate beneficiaries of the trust.

Because the grantor will no longer own the property that he has transferred into the trust, that property will not need to be probated. When the grantor dies, the person nominated as the "successor trustee" under the terms of the trust agreement will step into the grantor's shoes and will distribute the proceeds of the trust to the named beneficiaries in accordance with the terms of the trust agreement.

We will discuss revocable living trusts in greater detail in the next chapter.

Gifts During Your Lifetime

Giving away property while alive helps avoid probate, since anything that a person does not own when they die does not go through probate.

Probate Free Transfers of Assets

If the deceased owned motor vehicles or boats and their total value does not exceed a specified amount (varying from state to state, but usually between $25,000 to $75,000), ownership of these vehicles can be transferred probate free in most states to a surviving spouse/partner or other next of kin.

Additionally, any salary, wages, accumulated vacation and sick benefits, plus any other fringe benefits, may according to the laws of certain states be paid to the surviving spouse/partner, adult children or next of kin without the need for probate.

Simplified Transfer Procedures for "Small Estates"

If the deceased did not have any property to transfer, probate would not be necessary. The deceased's relatives may nonetheless decide to conduct probate proceedings if there are debts or taxes owed. This is done for the purpose of ensuring a proper wind up of the deceased's estate. If a decision is made to probate an estate for these specific reasons, it would be advisable to speak to an attorney to ascertain the best options available to you.

If a person does hold property at the time of death, generally it will be the size of his or her estate in monetary terms that will determine whether probate is required. Most states have adopted streamlined and simplified probate procedures for what is called the transfer of "small estates," with the limitation currently ranging from estates with net values of as low as $500 to as high as $500,000. If the deceased's estate is under this permitted limit, a simple certification procedure can be used instead of normal probate, thereby avoiding a lengthy and costly probate administration procedure. However, as most people generally have a home or land valued over the designated amount, few people can avail of this exemption from the probate process.

CHAPTER 9 | # Revocable Living Trusts

What Are Living Trusts?

A revocable living trust is a particular type of "inter vivos" trust (a trust made between living people) that is used for estate planning purposes. It is a written agreement created for the simple purpose of holding ownership of assets outside of your probate estate during your lifetime, and then distributing these assets to named beneficiaries after your death.

Specifically, you as the creator of the living trust (known as the "grantor") transfer property from your personal ownership to a trust that you have created. You then name yourself as the initial trustee of that trust. The result is that while legal ownership of the trust property changes from you to the trust, you (as initial trustee) continue to maintain control over your property and can continue to enjoy it in same way as you did prior to transferring it to the trust. When you die, a person appointed by you and known as a "successor trustee" (which is a little like an executor) steps in, takes control of the trust and transfers the trust assets to the people named as beneficiaries under the trust agreement.

Living trusts can be stated to be revocable, meaning that you as the grantor reserve the right to revoke or terminate the trust and resume personal ownership of the trust property at any time. In addition, you maintain discretionary rights to add to or withdraw assets from the trust property, to change the terms of the trust, and even to make it irrevocable at some time in the future.

Important Note

Not everyone needs a living trust. As a general rule of thumb, you might conclude that you do not need a living trust where you are young and healthy, you can more easily transfer your assets (or some of them) by other probate avoidance methods, or where you do not own any (or very little) property of value. So, consider your own situation carefully before making any decision to create a living trust.

Advantages of Living Trusts

There are several advantages to using living trusts. These include the following:

1. **Avoids probate**

    The main advantage of a living trust is that by transferring assets out of your name and into that of the trust, the assets will no longer be deemed to be part of your estate. As such, when you die there is no need to have these assets go through the probate process before they can be transferred to your beneficiaries. This allows for a quick distribution of your assets by your successor trustee to the beneficiaries named in your trust agreement.

2. **Saves money**

    By avoiding probate, you will also save your heirs a substantial amount of money in filing fees, costs, attorney fees and executor fees.

3. **Avoids publicity**

    With probate, your will (together with a schedule of all your assets) is filed in the probate registry and becomes a public document open for inspection by anyone upon payment of a small fee. By contrast, a living trust is essentially a private contract entered into between you (as grantor) and you (as trustee); and as there is no public filing requirement, details of your assets and the beneficiaries of those assets can remain confidential.

4. **Provides protection during incapacity**

A growing number of older people are transferring their assets into living trusts because they want to avoid them being placed under the management of a court-appointed guardian if they become unable to manage their affairs. With a properly drafted living trust, if you become disabled or otherwise unable to manage your estate, your living trust avoids the need for a court-mandated conservatorship by nominating a person known as a successor trustee (similar to a guardian) to manage the trust assets during any period of incapacity.

5. **Difficult to contest**

One of the often-overlooked benefits of a living trust is that its privacy makes it much more difficult to contest by comparison to a will. As the contents of a living trust are not publicly known, unlike wills which are available to the public for inspection, attorneys are less likely to spend their own time and money pursuing a lawsuit with unknown probabilities of success.

6. **Management of children's inheritance**

If you are concerned about the future welfare of your children, you can set up one or more separate child sub-trusts within your living trust for the benefit of each child should you die before they reach an age where they can take care of property themselves. The terms of the sub-trust will ordinarily provide that the child will not inherit the property from the sub-trust until he or she reaches a specified age of your choosing. Until the child or children reach the designated age, the successor trustee will manage the trust property on their behalf in accordance with the terms of the living trust.

You can also appoint a custodian under the UTMA to hold and manage assets on behalf of a child beneficiary until that beneficiary reaches an age specified by you in the trust agreement, which will be between 18 and 25 years depending on your state's law.

7. **Flexible**

Living trusts are extremely flexible. You can change the terms of the trust, add, and withdraw assets, change the beneficiaries of those assets, change the successor trustee, or even terminate the trust at any time.

Disadvantages of Living Trusts

There are several disadvantages to using living trusts. These include the following:

1. **Potential for failure to properly fund the living trust**

    One of the biggest problems associated with living trusts is the failure to properly transfer assets into the trust itself. This act of transferring assets is commonly referred to as "funding the trust." Where the assets are not properly transferred to the trust, they remain part of your probate estate and are not subject to the terms of your trust. If you have not provided for the transfer of these assets under your will, which is likely, they may end up being unintentionally gifted to the person entitled to the residue of your estate under your will or, where there is no will, to a relative on intestacy.

    If any of the assets you propose transferring to your trust have forms of "title documents" associated with them, you must ensure that the title is properly transferred from your personal name into the name of the trustee, acting as such on behalf of the trust (See "Title to Assets Transferred to a Living Trust" below).

2. **Does not completely avoid delays in distribution of assets**

    One of the principal reasons for delays in the probate process is caused by the necessity to resolve complicated tax issues before distributing assets to the beneficiaries of the deceased person's estate. An executor of your estate will not be inclined to carry out all your required distributions under your will until he knows the full extent of your tax liability. This unfortunately can take up to eighteen months in some instances to determine and resolve. More unfortunate, however, is the fact that the same problem exists equally in relation to a living trust, as a person is taxed as if the living trust does not exist. In other words, while for probate purposes the living trust owns the assets that have been transferred to it, for tax purposes you will still be deemed to own the assets in the living trust personally.

    Another common problem stems from the collection of assets, in particular life insurance proceeds. It can take months to obtain these proceeds, and again the problem exists both for an executor appointed under a will and a successor trustee appointed under a living trust.

    So while a living trust is not going to eliminate delays caused by tax issues or the collection of certain assets, it can speed up the distribution process in respect of other assets due to the lack of court intervention over the acts of the successor trustee. This should therefore go some way towards quickening the distribution process.

3. **Lack of court supervision**

    One of the benefits of the probate system is that the court often watches over the distribution of your estate, and in doing so protects the interests of your beneficiaries. However, no such supervision occurs with a living trust as the responsibility for effecting and overseeing the distribution of your trust assets rests solely with your designated successor trustee. This can be disadvantageous in certain circumstances.

4. Limited financial savings for smaller estates

The real determination as to whether a living trust will save you money depends on the amount of probate fees that would have been paid had the trust assets gone through probate rather than passing through your living trust. If the estate has a small monitory value, you may find that the probate fees payable in your state of residence are quite low in relation to the costs of establishing and maintaining a living trust.

5. No protection from creditors

Depending on state law, a revocable living trust will not ordinarily protect the trust assets from your creditors. In the same way as trusts are transparent for tax reasons, your creditors have a right to go after those assets as if they were still legally in your name.

There are some exceptions to the general principle above. The placing of assets into an "irrevocable" living trust before you incurred the debt in question can sometimes prohibit a creditor from suing the trust. However, the problem with irrevocable living trusts is that you cannot get the assets back yourself either. While a revocable living trust becomes irrevocable when you die, protection from your creditors may or may not be afforded to the assets that are contained in the trust—it will depend on the state in question and the circumstances surrounding the placing of assets in the trust in the first instance.

One of the principal drawbacks from not going through the probate process is that no time limit is imposed on creditors within which they can make claims against your estate. With probate, all creditors must notify the executor of any claim they have within a specified time limit. If they fail to notify the executor on time, their claim becomes barred by statute and they cannot recover against the estate or your trust. The opposite is the case with living trusts. No time limit is imposed on your creditors, and as such they can make claims against the assets in the trust at any time after you have died. Moreover, even when the trust is wound up and the assets distributed to the beneficiaries of the trust, they have the right in many states to sue the beneficiaries for the debts you owed—up to the maximum of the benefit the individual beneficiary received.

For the above reason, it is often quite useful to have some assets go through the probate process to restrict the rights of creditors to act against your estate and your trust.

The Role of the Initial Trustee

When it comes to living trusts, you will usually appoint yourself as the initial trustee of the trust. Where there are two grantors, such as in the case of a shared or joint trust (discussed in detail below), both grantors are usually appointed as co-trustees. Allowing grantors to serve as the initial trustees is a key feature of revocable living trusts, as the whole purpose behind a living trust is to bypass probate in a manner which allows you the right to retain complete freedom to deal with and control your assets.

You may of course decide either at the outset or later that you would prefer to nominate someone else to act as trustee of the trust. That is perfectly fine as the trustee will be obliged to act in accordance with your instructions as grantor of the trust—provided the instructions are legal. However, if someone else is acting as trustee of your trust, they will need to obtain an identification number from the Internal Revenue Service (IRS) for the trust and thereafter make income tax returns on behalf of the trust. We recommend that you see a lawyer if you choose not to act as trustee of your own trust. The removal of day-to-day control over your assets could have significant legal and practical consequences.

However, from a practical perspective, given that you were able to manage your assets and affairs while the assets were in your name, there is no reason why you cannot manage them as trustee. The reality is that as trustee of your own revocable trust you do not really owe any duties to anyone apart from yourself. As such, you can simply carry on managing your affairs as you always have provided you do not breach the terms of the trust.

It is important to note that you do not need to file any special tax returns on behalf of the trust. You simply report any income the trust property generates with your own income tax return in the same way that you always did.

Appointing a Co-Trustee

You may decide, for whatever reason, that rather than hand over the management of your trust assets to another person entirely, you would simply like to engage someone to assist in the management of your trust property. You can do this quite easily by appointing someone as a co-trustee of your trust. As co-trustees, both of you would have authority to act on the trust's behalf. Again, while there is no real difficulty with having someone else act as trustee of your trust or having someone act as a co-trustee, we recommend that you speak to a lawyer before you do this, as the terms of your trust document may need to be tailored to having someone other than yourself as a trustee.

Successor Trustees

Your successor trustee is the person who assumes control of the trust after you, as initial trustee, become incapacitated or die. In the case of a shared or joint trust, your successor trustee will take over control of the trust when both trustees are incapacitated or dead. A successor trustee has no authority to act while any of the grantors remain alive and capable of managing the trust. Your trust deed will identify the person or persons who will act as successor trustee(s) of your trust. In most cases, this is usually a relative or a family friend.

It is important to note that even though you name someone in the trust agreement to act as successor trustee, he or she is under absolutely no obligation to carry out the role and cannot be forced to do so. If anyone named as the successor trustee declines to act, the next named successor trustee will take over the management and administration of the trust. If no alternate is named or none of the named alternates are willing to serve, the beneficiaries of the trust will need to petition the local court to appoint someone to fill the role unless they have authority under the trust agreement to appoint a replacement successor trustee.

One of the most important aspects of your living trust is your choice of successor trustee(s). Do not choose a trustee just because they are a family member or close friend. Choose someone that you trust implicitly; someone that you know is competent and capable of handling the demands of a successor trustee's role. You also need to choose someone who is honestly willing to do the job for you. There is not much point in having to almost force someone into doing it. They need to be happy and ready to accept the task, and if they are not, they are most likely not the right candidate for the job.

The Role of the Successor Trustee

A successor trustee takes control of a living trust under two circumstances: the incapacity of the grantor and the death of the grantor. We will look at each in turn.

Role of Successor Trustee During the Incapacity of the Grantor

The first thing your successor trustee will need to do will be to locate the living trust agreement. Normally, a living trust agreement will contain a clear set of instructions for determining whether the grantor is incapacitated or not. Often, the terms of the trust will require one or sometimes two doctors (which we recommend) to certify that the grantor is unable to comprehend or to competently manage his affairs. Once the doctors certify incapacitation, the successor trustee stands in and takes control of the trust property.

Next, your successor trustee must ensure that you are in receipt of appropriate medical attention.

Usually, the terms of a living trust will allow for the successor trustee to apply an element of the trust assets towards your care and welfare. If you have no insurance or assets outside the trust to fund that medical care, it is important that the successor trustee acts with the utmost haste.

If you have any children or dependents, your successor trustee will also need to arrange for their care. There should be specific instructions in the living trust to deal with such matters. Also, if you have any assets, your successor trustee will need to manage them so that their value is preserved. Finally, your successor trustee will need to obtain a taxpayer identification number and file annual income tax returns for your revocable trust.

Hopefully, you will recover from your incapacity. If you do, everything goes back to normal as the successor trustee no longer needs to act on your behalf.

Role of Successor Trustee Following the Death of the Grantor

When you, the grantor, die, it becomes your successor trustee's responsibility to assume control of the trust estate and administer it in accordance with the terms of the living trust agreement. The administration process involves the collection of assets, payment of debts and taxes, and the distribution of assets to the ultimate beneficiaries of the living trust. In most cases these beneficiaries will be your partner, spouse and/or children, but as the grantor you have the right to pass your trust assets to virtually anyone. Keep in mind, however, that spouses have certain rights, so if you are married your freedom will be somewhat restricted.

In any event, let us take a brief look at the tasks performed by a successor trustee during the "administration" process.

1. Obtain certified copies of the death certificate

One of your successor trustee's first tasks following your death will be to procure copies of your death certificate. The certificate, together with an Affidavit of Trust, should be presented to third parties (courts, banks, financial institutions, insurance companies, etc.) in order to establish that the successor trustee is lawfully entitled to deal with the trust assets.

A death certificate can generally be obtained from the state's Office of Vital Records or from the Department of Health, but there are some variations from state to state. The successor trustee could also contact your general practitioner or funeral director, each of whom should be able to procure a copy of your death certificate.

2. Obtain a tax identification number for the trust

Next, your successor trustee will need to make an application to the IRS to obtain a tax identification number for the trust. The application can be made using the IRS Form 1041 (https://www.irs.gov/forms-pubs/about-form-1041).

3. Collection and management of trust assets

Having obtained a death certificate and made an Affidavit of Trust (which will be required when dealing with the trust assets), the next task for your successor trustee is to take possession of the trust's assets and to evaluate what debts, claims, taxes, and other expenses will be payable by the trust. Your successor trustee should work very closely with the executor of your estate to determine what assets have been transferred into the trust.

Important Note

An Affidavit of Trust is a declaration sworn by you in front of a notary public confirming that you are the trustee of the trust, with relevant pages of the trust attached to evidence your appointment as trustee. You will require an Affidavit of Trust when dealing with banks and other financial institutions. Your successor trustee will also need to make a similar affidavit in due course.

Often, a Certification of Trust can be used instead of an Affidavit of Trust. It is the same as an Affidavit of Trust except it does not need to be notarized.

Your successor trustee should commence the process by reviewing the trust agreement and trust records to establish what assets have been transferred into the trust and what debts might exist. It is important that your successor trustee secures the assets. Securities (especially bearer bonds), title deeds, jewelry, and other items of substantial value should be physically located and placed in a safe deposit box or safe. Other assets should be insured as appropriate against risks such as fire, damage, theft, loss, and liability. Once the assets are secured, the successor trustee should proceed to obtain a valuation of all assets as well as an assessment of any liabilities incurred by the trust.

In addition, as part of the collection and management of trust assets, your successor trustee should carry out the actions set out below.

Claim life insurance proceeds

Your successor trustee should contact any insurance company with whom you as the grantor held a life insurance policy. If the living trust was named as a designated beneficiary on that policy, then your successor trustee should make a claim for any insurance proceeds due to the trust.

Gain access to bank accounts and other financial accounts

Each financial institution that held an account for the trust should be notified of your death so as to commence the process of releasing control of the proceeds of the accounts to the successor trustee and/or the trust beneficiary.

Identify debts owed by the grantor

As mentioned, your successor trustee should ensure that any valid debts against the trust are discharged from the trust assets.

Maintain proper accountings of trust assets

Your successor trustee will have a duty to prepare an annual accounting in respect of the trust assets (unless the beneficiaries waive their rights to such an accounting). The accounting should display the assets held by the trust at the date of your death as well as current market valuations. The accounting should also include any income received, any expenditure made, and any assets added to or taken out of the trust. To prepare this, the successor trustee will need to keep meticulous records of all disbursements from the trust.

4. Preparing and filing tax returns

The successor trustee and the executor of your estate are collectively responsible for the payment of the various taxes set out below.

Federal estate tax

As trusts are transparent for tax purposes, the extent of your assets, both inside and outside the trust, will need to be appraised following your death. If the value of your assets exceeds the estate tax threshold, then estate tax will become payable on the excess. It is the responsibility of your successor trustee and your executor to determine if estate tax is due, and then to prepare and file the appropriate tax return and pay any taxes that are owed using the assets in your estate.

Income taxes

A final income tax return will need to be made for the final year of your life. The return should be made on IRS Form 1040. Again, the payment of tax should be coordinated between the successor trustee and the executor.

Trust income tax returns

Following your death, all income generated by your trust will need to be accounted for to the IRS. The return for the trust will be made on IRS Form 1041 for each calendar year. It is the sole responsibility of the successor trustee to ensure that these returns are made. If your living trust is a shared trust (described below), two separate tax returns will need to be made after your death.

State taxes and pick-up taxes

Finally, your successor trustee and executor will also need to discharge any state taxes or pick-up taxes that may be owed by your estate.

5.   Transferring property to beneficiaries

Once all the assets have been identified and gathered, and all debts and taxes paid or provided for, the successor trustee can distribute the remaining trust assets in accordance with the terms of the living trust. The assets will either be distributed in cash or in kind if the trust includes specific tangible assets.

To properly carry out the distribution, the beneficiaries will need to have the trust assets re-registered in their names by the successor trustee. As such, the successor trustee will need to go through the process for transferring title in the trust assets over to the beneficiaries. After the re-registration, the assets are deemed effectively transferred to the beneficiaries of the trust. In each case, the successor trustee should have each beneficiary sign an acknowledgement to confirm that he or she has received the distribution in question.

6.   Administering a child's trust

The duties of the successor normally terminate once he has distributed the trust assets to the beneficiaries of the trust. However, where the grantor has created a sub-trust for any of his children or indeed any other child in the living trust, the successor trustee will need to continue acting as trustee if he has been named trustee of the child's trust. In essence, he or she will need to manage the trust assets left to the child until such time as the child, or children if there is more than one, reaches the age specified in the trust agreement. This will greatly add to the task of the successor trustee, as he or she will need to ensure that the trust assets are properly invested and secured for the period of the child's trust, as well as make provision from time to time for the welfare, upkeep and education of the child. Only when the last child reaches the age specified in the trust document can the successor trustee formally distribute the remaining assets and wind down the living trust. This may well be years or even decades after the grantor has died.

7.   Winding down the trust

The length of time that it takes to settle the trust and distribute assets is often dependent on whether an estate tax return is due. If a return will be due, then it is typically prudent to wait until after a closing letter is received from the IRS to make final distributions. This can take up to 18 months—or more if the estate is audited—after the date of the grantor's death to receive. However, if no estate tax is due, the trust can usually be wrapped up in several months; assuming of course that there are no on-going trusts established under the terms of the living trust itself.

Fiduciary Duties of the Successor Trustee

While it is not within the scope of this book to provide a comprehensive list of a successor trustee's duties, it is useful for you to have an understanding of their role and duties so that you can decide who is best for the role. As with the executor of your estate, the successor trustee of your living trust owes the beneficiaries of the trust a fiduciary duty.

Some specific fiduciary duties of a successor trustee include the duty to:

- Adhere to the terms of the trust.
- Act personally in the management and administration of the trust.
- Act in the best interests of the beneficiaries of the trust.
- Supply annual reports as well as information regarding the trust and its assets to the beneficiaries.
- Invest prudently.
- Keep trust assets separate from those of the successor trustee.
- Carry out the role of trustee without payment—unless the terms of the trust provide otherwise, or the trustee is a professional trustee.

Changing Trustees

While you are alive, you can amend the trust agreement to change the proposed trustee at any time. However, to provide for a possible change of trustees after your death, specific provisions will need to be inserted into your trust deed. For example, to cover the possibility that a successor trustee wishes to resign, you should include provisions to ensure an orderly transition from the resigning trustee to the successor trustee. In this regard, you could require that the resignation of a trustee will not become effective until at least fourteen to thirty days after written notice of the resignation has been given to you if still alive, or to the trust's beneficiaries if you are dead. These notice requirements will ensure that you or the beneficiaries of the trust have sufficient time to have a successor trustee in place before the resigning trustee resigns.

If a beneficiary of your trust, on the other hand, is either unhappy or concerned about the manner in which a successor trustee is dealing with the trust property, and the situation cannot be resolved by discussion between them, he or she will have the option of petitioning the court to effect the removal of the successor trustee. However, in the absence of having just cause, the beneficiary will find it extremely difficult to remove the successor trustee.

The Beneficiaries of Your Living Trust

The beneficiaries of a trust are almost identical to those of a will. Therefore, we will only review in general certain matters pertinent to living trust beneficiaries. For full detailed information on beneficiaries, please refer to Chapter 2 or to our book, *"Make Your Own Living Trust & Avoid Probate."*

Let us have a brief look at of the types of beneficiaries you can have for your living trust:

- **Primary Beneficiaries** are those whom you name to receive specific property. These beneficiaries include individuals, institutions, and groups.

- **Alternate Beneficiaries** are the ones you name to get property left initially to a primary beneficiary who has predeceased you or refused the gift.

- **Residuary beneficiaries** are those who will receive all the property of the trust not left to either primary or alternate beneficiaries.

Should you wish to change beneficiaries, it is a simple matter to amend the trust and add or remove names. If you wish, you can also name specific alternate beneficiaries for each gift made to a primary beneficiary. The alternate beneficiary will take the gift if the primary beneficiary predeceases you or refuses to accept the gift.

If you wish, you can include a "no-contest clause" in your living trust. This is a condition placed in a living trust (or will for that matter) which is used to discourage beneficiaries from trying to claim more than you have left them. Under a no-contest clause, a beneficiary who challenges the terms of your living trust (most likely because he or she wants more than you have left them) loses all his or her inheritance under that document.

Types of Living Trust

The two main types of living trusts used for estate planning purposes are basic living trusts and AB Trusts. A basic living trust, which can be used by an individual or a couple, has the primary objective of avoiding probate. An AB Trust, on the other hand, goes one step further by saving on estate taxes. We will discuss each of these types of trust in more detail below.

Living Trust for an Individual

If you are single, you probably want your living trust to transfer your property to your relatives and friends following your death. If this is the case, then the basic living trust could be right for you. As already explained, to create a basic living trust you simply sign a trust agreement between yourself as grantor and yourself as trustee. Under the terms of the trust agreement you will nominate someone to act as your successor trustee and specify who is to receive the benefit of your trust assets following your death. When you die, your successor trustee steps in and transfers the trust property to the beneficiaries named in your living trust.

Important Tip

Remember that to appoint a testamentary guardian to care for your minor children following your death, you will need to make that appointment in your will. You cannot do this in your trust.

If you have any children, you can use your living trust to leave property to them; with care of that property being vested in a property guardian or trustee until they reach the age you have specified in your trust agreement.

Living Trusts for Couples

Couples, whether married or not, often own property together. If you are part of a couple, you can decide whether you want to create an individual trust for your own separate property or whether you want to create a joint or shared living trust with your partner.

If you are married, then you will need to consider whether you are living in a community property state or whether you are living in a common law state. Depending on what state you are living in, the law will determine what is deemed your individual property and what is deemed joint marital (community) property. You can transfer your individual property to a living trust as well as your share of your community property.

There are four principal types of living trust arrangement that couples can create:

- Each spouse or partner prepares their own individual living trust.
- Both of you prepare one shared living trust.
- Both of you prepare a basic AB trust.
- Both of you prepare an AB disclaimer trust.

We discuss each arrangement in detail below.

Individual Living Trusts

For couples, the use of individual trusts can make a lot of sense where you and your spouse/partner own most of your property separately rather than jointly. In such cases, you may want to ensure that your spouse does not gain control over your assets once you transfer them to the trust while at the same time ensuring that your assets are not tied up in probate. An individual trust is ideal in such circumstances.

However, there are drawbacks to using individual living trusts. For example, in order to transfer a jointly held asset into a trust, it may become necessary to divide the title to the asset into two separate deeds and thereafter have each spouse transfer their half of the asset to their trust. This can become expensive and messy, and sometimes in such circumstances it makes sense to create an additional trust to hold the jointly held assets. For this reason, it is often recommended that married couples or couples in a registered partnership avoid individual trusts in favor of shared living trusts. Of course, the choice is yours.

Basic Shared Living Trusts

Many couples use one basic shared living trust to avoid probate and to handle both their co-owned property and their separately held property. Here, both partners establish the trust and act as co-grantors and co-trustees of the trust. As co-grantors, each partner can nominate beneficiaries for their separate property and for their portion of the joint property. In addition, each partner can unilaterally call for the return of their assets to them and/or revoke the trust at any time. When the trust is revoked, the assets return to the parties that placed them in the trust. In that case, each partner regains full ownership and control of all their separate property as well as their share of the jointly owned property.

When one of the partners dies, the trust automatically splits into two separate trusts—we will call them the "first trust" and the "second trust." The deceased partner's separate property and share of the joint property is automatically transferred into the first trust, with the surviving partner's separate property and share of the joint property going into the second trust. The terms of the first trust immediately become irrevocable, which means the surviving partner cannot amend them in any way. Thereafter, the surviving partner in his/her capacity as successor trustee distributes the property in the first trust in accordance with the deceased partner's wishes as set out in the trust document. In many cases, the deceased partner will leave his or her assets to the surviving partner's trust—the second trust. The second trust is revocable by the surviving partner in the same way as an individual trust. When the surviving partner dies, the trust assets will be distributed in accordance with the terms of the trust agreement in the usual way.

Basic AB Trusts

Generally, one spouse or partner will leave their entire estate to the other spouse, partly to allow the survivor to have the benefit of their assets and partly because the transfer is initially tax-free due to the marital exclusion. However, if as a result of this transfer the value of the surviving spouse's estate ultimately ends up exceeding the individual tax exclusion amount ($13,990,000 in 2025) at the time of his or her death (See Chapter 11), then estate tax may be payable on the excess. This tax, or at least part of it, can be avoided with proper planning, and the use of an AB trust is one method that has in the past been used to achieve this.

An AB trust has previously been useful where the combined value of your estate and that of your spouse is likely to exceed the individual exclusion amount, which can vary from year to year (See Chapter 11 for a detailed discussion of estate taxes). For example, during the 2025 tax year, federal estate tax law provided that no tax would be assessed on a person's estate if the value of their taxable estate at death was worth less than the $13,990,000 exclusion amount. Where the value of that estate exceeded this amount, the excess was taxed at the rate of 40 percent.

With an AB trust, on the death of one of the spouses the trust splits into two separate trusts—"Trust A" and "Trust B." Assets equal to the value of the deceased spouse's individual exclusion amount are transferred to the deceased spouse's Trust B for the benefit of the beneficiaries, such as his or her children. The remainder of the trust assets is transferred to Trust A, for the benefit of the surviving spouse. Therefore, at the time the first spouse dies, no estate tax is payable because the amount going to Trust B uses up the available exclusion amount, and the amount going to Trust A takes advantage of the marital exemption for transfers to a surviving spouse.

The terms of the AB trust can also provide that the surviving spouse will become a "life beneficiary" of Trust B. As such, the survivor can have the use and benefit of the assets in Trust B for the rest of their life without being given complete ownership of any of it. The surviving spouse can therefore use all the income generated from the property in Trust B for his or her own support and upkeep but cannot sell the assets or deal with them in any way.

When the surviving spouse dies, all the trust property in both Trust A and Trust B is distributed to the beneficiaries in accordance with the terms of the AB Trust. The property in Trust B passes tax free because it was subject to the exclusion amount at the time the first spouse died and was never transferred to the surviving spouse and therefore is not part of his or her estate. The property in Trust A is now subject to estate tax before passing to the ultimate beneficiaries, but the second spouse to die can take advantage of his or her own exclusion amount to reduce or eliminate the amount that is subject to tax. This means that that if the exclusion amount of the second spouse to die covers the amount remaining in Trust A, then the beneficiaries of Trust A and Trust B, who are most likely the children of the couple, can receive the combined assets of the trusts tax-free.

Despite the benefits, there are several disadvantages associated with the use of AB living trusts, including:

- control over the property in Trust B may be restricted—the rights of the surviving spouse are limited to an entitlement to the interest or other income derived from the trust property, use of the trust property, and utilization of the trust property for the purpose of discharging costs incurred in connection with his or her health, education, support and maintenance.
- the spouses may need to pay legal or accounting fees to facilitate the division of property between the Trust A and Trust B.
- tax returns must be filed on behalf of Trust B.
- separate records must be kept regarding the trust property in each of the two trusts.
- because of the uncertain nature of estate taxes, you cannot be assured of any tax benefit (See "The Impact of 'Portability' on AB Trusts and AB Disclaimer Trusts" below).

AB Disclaimer Trust

An AB disclaimer trust works the same as the basic AB trust, apart from one very important factor—the surviving spouse has the right to determine how much, if any, property goes into Trust A at the time of the first spouse's death.

The AB disclaimer trust is a trust that names the surviving spouse as the beneficiary of the other spouse's estate (which is initially tax free in the normal course). However, the surviving spouse has the option of renouncing or disclaiming all or part of the trust assets which he or she is to receive from the deceased spouse.

The disclaimed assets would pass to a credit shelter trust (similar to Trust B for the Basic AB Trust discussed above) for the benefit of the named beneficiaries—with the surviving spouse having a life interest in these trust assets. However, if the assets are not disclaimed and are allowed to pass to Trust A for the benefit of the surviving spouse, he or she will have full control and "ownership" over them as if they were in an individual trust.

Again, and like the situation with an ordinary AB trust, the assets in both Trust A and Trust B will be distributed on the death of the surviving spouse.

The Impact of 'Portability' on AB Trusts and AB Disclaimer Trusts

AB Trusts and AB Disclaimer Trusts became popular during a time when the second spouse to die was not allowed to utilize any remaining portion of the first spouse to die's individual exclusion amount. However, as explained in Chapter 11, the surviving spouse is now allowed to use the remaining portion of his or her deceased spouse's exclusion amount, thus increasing the exclusion amount available to the surviving spouse up to a maximum of $13,990,000 in 2025—this estate planning rule and technique is called "portability." The new rules allowing for portability effectively accomplish most of what the AB Trust or AB Disclaimer Trust were trying to accomplish, and so some experts question whether these types of trusts are now obsolete.

However, there may be some specific circumstances where AB Trusts and AB Disclaimer Trusts are still beneficial. One scenario is where a couple resides in a state with its own death taxes, because no such state has yet adopted portability. It also may apply if you're in a second marriage and want to ensure that certain of your assets can be used by your current spouse after your death but then pass to your children from your first marriage upon your current spouse's death. After the advent of portability, however, while AB Trusts and AB Disclaimer Trusts may still be considered as an option on the estate planning menu, they will rarely be selected.

Conclusion

You should carefully consider the use of each of the above types of trust before deciding that any of them would suit your circumstances. Remember, each comes with its own set of advantages and disadvantages. You should choose wisely and tailor any living trust to your own unique circumstances.

Transferring Assets to Your Living Trust

As discussed previously, there are two primary reasons why you might establish a revocable living trust. Firstly, you want to provide for the management of your property during any period of incapacity. Secondly, you want to avoid the costs and delays associated with having your assets go through the probate process. Both are perfectly legitimate and solid reasons for establishing your living trust. However, if having established the trust you fail to properly transfer assets to the trust, or "fund" the trust as the term is called, your efforts will have been in vain. Without complying with the required formalities to transfer assets to your trust, these assets will be deemed to be your personal assets and will end up going through the probate process; or the intestate administration process if you have failed to make a last will and testament.

What Assets Should Be Put in Your Living Trust?

One of the principal goals of any living trust is to avoid the cost associated with probate, with the general rule being that the more an asset is worth, the more it will cost your estate on probate fees. It follows therefore that you should, at the very least, consider transferring your most valuable assets to your living trust. However, it is entirely up to you what you decide to include or leave out.

You are free to include assets such as your home and other real estate, bank and saving accounts, investments, business interests, antiques, jewelry, personal belongings, royalties, patents, copyrights, stocks, bonds and other securities, money market accounts and so on.

In deciding what assets you want to transfer to your living trust, always bear in mind that where you are acting as both the grantor and trustee of your own trust, you always have the right to call for the return of any assets you transfer into the trust.

The reality is that you do not need to put everything into your living trust to save money on probate. See the previous chapter for details of the items which do not go through the probate process.

There is no need to include these items in your living trust, as they will pass to the designated beneficiaries automatically and outside of the probate net.

Title to Assets Transferred to a Living Trust

A trust is not a legal entity—it is simply the legal relationship between the grantor and the trustee. Therefore, a trust cannot hold title to property such as real estate, bank accounts, etc. in its own name (the way a corporation can, for example). It is the trustee rather that must hold legal title to the trust assets, with the beneficiaries holding what is called "equitable" or beneficial title. Since the trustee holds legal title to the trust assets, those assets are always held in the trustee's name—albeit "as trustee" for the designated trust. So when we refer to assets being transferred to a trust, this means that legal title to those assets is being transferred to the trustee to be held in trust in accordance with the agreement between the grantor and the trustee.

To transfer assets which do not have title documents to your trust, all you typically need to do is simply list them in the schedule of assets contained at the back of your trust agreement. With respect to assets which do have title documents, while there has been considerable debate as to whether property transferred to a living trust is required to be re-titled in the name of the trustee (as trustee for the trust), we recommend that all assets which have any form of title document should be re-titled in this manner.

In order to change the title of an asset from your personal name to the name of the trustee for your living trust, you simply sign a document transferring the legal title in that asset from you to the trustee. The transfer will be between, for example, John Smith and John Smith, trustee of the John Smith Family living trust dated 1 January 2025. Then when it comes to signing the transfer document, you will sign the document in your own right as (for example) "John Smith" AND you will also sign on behalf of the living trust using the words "John Smith, Trustee."

Be aware, any failure to properly transfer the asset can result in its remaining as part of your probate estate.

Transferring Property to Your Trust

Given the vast diversity of assets that you can transfer to your living trust, we will take a very brief look below at some of the most commonly transferred assets and how those transfers should be effected so as to ensure that they become part of your trust estate.

Real Estate

To transfer real estate into your living trust you will need to prepare a deed of transfer. In most cases this can be straightforward. Be careful, however, because there are many nuances associated with the transfer of title to real estate—such as the type of deed required, title insurance, mortgages, out-of-state property, homestead rights and tax on transfer deeds. As such, we recommend that you engage the services of an attorney qualified in your state to assist with the transfer of any property located in your state.

Important Tip

Remember to notify your insurance company when transferring your personal property to a living trust.

Cars, Boats and Other Vehicles

You can transfer a vehicle to your trust in much the same way as you would transfer it to a third party. All you will need to do is contact the department of vehicles (or its website) to obtain the relevant forms, complete them and return them. It should be noted that most states have specific forms that need to be used for registering the transfer of vehicles and watercraft – so be sure to complete the correct one.

Cash Accounts

In order to transfer the title to your current (checking) accounts, savings accounts or money market accounts, you can either change the name on the account (e.g. from "John Smith" to "John Smith, trustee of John Smith Family living trust") or close the account and open a new one. Each relevant financial institution can advise on which of the two methods they will allow.

United States Savings Bonds

While U.S. Savings bonds can be transferred into your living trust, you will need to contact your bank to obtain the appropriate form to transfer the bonds as well as details of the procedure involved. Once the transfer is completed, the bonds will be re-issued in the name of the trustee on behalf of your living trust.

Broker Accounts

It is also possible to transfer a broker account held with a brokerage firm or with a mutual fund company to your living trust. Similar to the position with bank accounts, you will need to contact the firm/company to determine whether they can simply change the name on the account or whether they will have to close the existing account and open a new one in the name of the trustee (on behalf of the trust).

Publicly Quoted Stocks

There are two ways to transfer stock in a publicly quoted company to your living trust. You can contact the company's share registrar (or "transfer agent" as it's often called) or you can contact your broker and ask him to open an account in the name of the trustee (on behalf of the trust) and have the stock re-issued to the trustee.

Retirement Plans

Due to their complexity, tax advantages and unique distribution features, pension plans, profit-sharing plans, IRSs, Keoghs, SEPs and other qualified pension plans should never be transferred into a living trust without first consulting your tax advisor. As such, be sure to consult your tax advisor before making any purported transfer of such plans to your living trust.

Other Property

If you want to transfer any other property to your living trust, a simple deed of assignment should suffice. However, if there are specific documents required to effect transfers of property (such as share transfer forms for a corporation) then you should use the required form. If you are uncertain as to how to proceed, we suggest that you contact an attorney.

Finally, remember you can transfer assets out of your living trust and back to you by simply reversing the process outlined above. As grantor and trustee, you ordinarily have full authority and capacity to do this.

Revocation of Your Living Trust

While it is not too common an occurrence, a living trust can be revoked at any time. To revoke a living trust, you must do the following:

- In your capacity as grantor, prepare and serve a notice of revocation on the trustee of the trust (which is generally the grantor). The notice will inform the trustee that the trust is terminated and will call for the return of the trust assets to the grantor. Note that in the case of a shared living trust or an AB Trust, notwithstanding that there are normally two co-grantors, either co-grantor alone is legally entitled to terminate the trust by serving a notice of revocation.

- Arrange for legal title in the trust assets to be transferred from the living trust back to the grantor personally.

- Ensure that any beneficiary designations in favor of the living trust are amended. In this respect, we are talking about pay-on-death accounts, life insurance, etc.

Pour-Over Wills

A pour-over will is a special type of will that is used in conjunction with a living trust. Instead of providing for the distribution of all of your assets and property, the pour-over will simply provides that any of your property that has not been transferred into your living trust before your death will "pour-over" into your living trust after you die. In this way, it ensures that these assets will be distributed in accordance with the provisions set out in your living trust.

In essence, a pour-over will is like most other wills. It provides for the revocation of other wills, names an executor, and appoints a guardian for minor children. The one real difference is that it has one specific beneficiary—your living trust.

While a pour-over will has certain advantages, the major drawback is that the property passing under the will may have to go through probate. This in turn means that the beneficiaries of your living trust must wait for probate to complete before the assets are transferred to the trust. They will also have to wait for the successor trustee to make the subsequent distribution from the living trust. The chances of a speedy distribution in those circumstances are slim unless the grantor's probate estate outside the living trust is small enough to avail of the expedited procedures available for the probate of "small estates."

Notwithstanding the above, the use of a pour-over will can be beneficial where circumstances exist which deter people from putting all their property into their living trusts during their lifetimes. For example, due to restrictions imposed by certain states and insurance companies, it can often be difficult to buy, sell, or insure assets held in a living trust.

In other situations, people who have established living trusts simply forget to transfer all their assets to the trust or don't get an opportunity to do so. For example, someone might have received an inheritance a few days before they die and simply never had an opportunity during their last days to make the transfer.

The use of a pour-over will is therefore a good means to avoid intestacy and having state law determine how your assets should be divided. Similarly, there is no reason why you cannot simply have a will of your own with a standard residuary clause similar to that set out in the living trust—it more or less accomplishes the same thing in most instances. However, there may be situations under the terms of a living trust where the residuary trust estate is passed to a minor beneficiary and a sub-trust is set up to provide for the management of the child's property until he or she is old enough to take control of the property. In such circumstances, it makes sense to flow the excess assets into the living trust rather than providing for a separate trust for the same child under the terms of your will.

All in all, it is fair to say that whenever a living trust is used, it can be wise to have a pour-over will to cover assets not transferred to the trust.

Resource

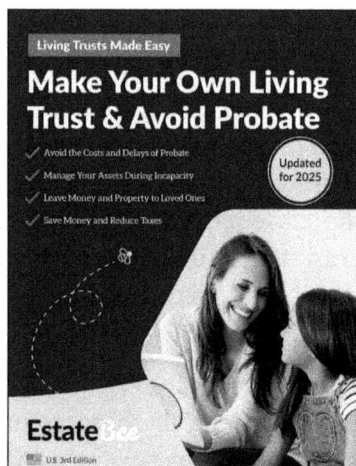

For further information on assets that do not go through probate, see **Make Your Own Living Trust & Avoid Probate**

Living trusts are used to distribute a person's assets after they die in a manner that avoids the costs, delays, and publicity of probate. They also cater for the management of property during periods of incapacity.

This book will guide you step-by-step through the process of creating your very own living trust, transferring assets to your living trust, and subsequently managing those assets. All relevant forms are included.

Get your copy at **www.estate-bee.com/product/make-your-own-living-trust-avoid-probate/**

CHAPTER 10

Educational Trusts and Pet Trusts

Educational Trusts

An educational trust is established to provide funds for the beneficiary's education. Parents are not the only persons who can set up an educational trust. In fact, anyone can set up and be the grantor of an educational trust—e.g. a parent, grandparent, aunt or uncle, close friend of the family, etc.—as long as that person holds an interest in the education of the person for whom the trust will support.

You can fund an educational trust by contributions of cash and/or property. The funds and any proceeds received from the trust's use of the funds (e.g. interest or an increase in the value of securities) are then used to provide for education-related expenses such as tuition, books, living expenses, transportation, etc. A trustee (usually yourself while alive and someone you designate to take over after your death) manages the trust and distributes the funds to the beneficiary according to your specific instructions as grantor.

For example, you can specify in the trust document exactly what type of education the trust funds can be used to pay for. As such, you can name the type of educational institution that is acceptable—such as a university, graduate school, trade school, community college, etc. In any event, it is important to leave your successor trustee clear instructions as to what kind of education may be funded and the allowable uses of funds.

An educational trust can be either a "living trust," which is created and funded during the lifetime of the grantor, or a testamentary trust, which is established by a provision in a will and funded at the time of the grantor's death.

A living trust, the most common form of educational trust, has the advantage of avoiding probate with respect to the money and other property contributed to the trust. This saves the time and money involved with probate, ensures the funds will not be hung-up during that time, and maintains privacy since living trusts are not publicly available documents.

A testamentary trust is created through a provision of your will. This means that the funds involved will be required to go through probate and will be subject to the related time and costs involved. In addition, the terms of the trust will be publicly available. However, gifts transferred to a trust because of your death are not subject to a gift tax. In addition, you do not have to fund the trust while you are still alive. For obvious reasons, a testamentary educational trust works best when small children are involved, and the grantor is towards the end of his or her life.

You can set up separate educational trusts for each of your children or one trust for all of them. If you set up one trust for multiple children, however, you will have to decide and state how the trustee should distribute the funds among the beneficiaries, whether by percentage, the trustee's discretion, or some other formula.

By its terms, setting up an educational trust begs many questions that must be answered and provided for, such as:

- What happens if the beneficiary does not want the education—e.g. a university education—specified in the trust document?
- What happens if the beneficiary has another source of funding—e.g. a scholarship—and does not need some or all the money for educational purposes?
- What if the beneficiary dies?
- When does the educational trust terminate?
- What happens to any leftover funds in the trust once it terminates?

In the terms of your trust, you will need to consider these scenarios and make plans for them. For example, you may decide that if there is still money in the trust when the beneficiary reaches a certain age, then it should be made available to a different beneficiary.

As you can see, the main advantage of an educational trust is control. As grantor, you can specify to whom, for what purposes, and in what manner the funds are to be disbursed, and the trustee (who will most likely be you until you die, and a responsible adult who you trust afterwards) controls those disbursements according to the terms of the trust. In addition, any trustee holds a fiduciary responsibility to the beneficiary of the trust fund and must administer the trust in good faith and in accordance with the terms of the trust document and applicable laws. Finally, the beneficiary normally has little or no direct access to the proceeds of the trust—at least until he or she reaches a certain age.

You can also specify when the money will become available. One way is to say the beneficiary must reach a certain age or achieve specified milestones. Once he or she becomes eligible for the funds, they can be disbursed in one lump sum, over set periods of time, or based on any formula you choose.

All of this ensures that the child, as the beneficiary, cannot carelessly spend the money that has been set aside for his or her education. In addition, if the educational trust is properly established, then creditors of the grantor or the beneficiary are unable to receive payment out of the trust for a debt unrelated to the purpose of the trust.

Another advantage of an educational trust is that the cash and property you contribute to the trust are not considered part of your estate and therefore are not subject to estate tax when you die. In addition, making gifts to an educational trust not only removes the assets contributed to the trust from your estate, but it also removes any interest, dividends, or appreciation generated by those assets, which could be significant especially if you begin contributing to the trust when your child is of a young age.

Be aware, however, that there are potential gift taxes involved with contributions to educational living trusts, which need to be understood before establishing and funding such a trust. In addition, there may be state and/or federal taxes on the earnings of the trust. But there are ways to help minimize those taxes, which is another reason why we recommend that you consult a professional financial and/or legal advisor when setting up an educational trust.

Finally, before setting up an educational trust, you should become familiar with your "education savings plan" options, such as a 529 Education Savings Plan and a Coverdell Education Savings Account.

Educational savings plans are subject to strict requirements under federal and state tax codes, and the funds belong to the contributor until they are distributed to the student. In general, unless the amount you wish to set aside for your child's education exceeds $100,000, an education savings plan will probably be easier to establish and offer greater tax savings than an educational trust.

Pet Trusts

If you are a pet lover, then your pet is probably a genuine part of your family. As such, you will want to make sure that if anything happens to you, then your pet will be well provided for and cared for. However, pets cannot own property so you cannot leave your pet money in your will. But you do have range of options available to make sure that:

- your pet goes to a caring person or organization, and
- the new caretaker has the resources to take good care of your beloved friend.

Before selecting one of these options, you need to find a person or organization that you trust to care for your pet and verify that person or organization is willing to do so.

In addition, be aware that only legally enforceable documents, such as a will or a pet trust, can guarantee a good life for your pet if you die or become incapacitated. Even well-meaning promises by family and friends to take care of your pets often do not meet the test of the reality of doing so.

Can I Provide for My Pet Under a Will?

As mentioned earlier, you cannot directly bequeath money or property to your pet under your will. If your will says that you leave assets to your pet, those assets will simply go into your residuary estate. In addition, because a pet is itself considered property, if you do not leave your pet to a specific caretaker, your pet will become part of the residuary as well. If you have not made a will, all your property, including your pet, will be distributed through intestate succession according to the laws of your state.

However, you can use your will to leave both your pet and the resources necessary to properly care for your pet to a designated caretaker. The financial problem with this approach is that the amount you leave for your pet's care could be subject to estate tax. The practical problem is that the caretaker will have no legally enforceable obligation to either use the money on behalf of your pet, or to care for your pet in the manner you instruct.

However, forty states and the District of Columbia do recognize "statutory pet trusts," whereby pet owners who include a simple directive in their will can be assured that the funds and pet will remain together. In the ten states without statutory pet trusts, however, these provisions are "honorary" and not legally enforceable.

In addition, because your will must pass through probate, there will be a waiting period before your pet and the money designated to care for your pet becomes the property of your designated caretaker. If the will is challenged, this period may be even longer. Finally, a will cannot address the possibility that your pet may need to be cared for if you become incapacitated.

Setting Up a Pet Trust

The best option to provide for your pet is to make a pet trust—although this is the most expensive option as well. A pet trust allows you to avoid most of the pitfalls of a will: the money you leave to care for your pet does not go through probate and therefore is not subject to delay and challenge; and the caretaker will have a legal obligation to care for your pet.

In fact, the creation of a pet trust is much the same as most types of trusts. You need to decide how and when you will fund the trust, when it will become operational, what will happen to the remaining trust assets when the pet dies, and who will act as trustee. You will also need to identify the caretaker and any alternates should they not be able or not want to perform their duties. Finally, you should include specific instructions for the care of your pet.

The same person or organization named as the pet's caretaker can also be the trustee in charge of the funds but appointing a different person or organization to each role protects the pets and the funds you left behind. Many factors should be considered when deciding how much to leave for a pet's care, including the fact that pets are more expensive as they age. Another thing to keep in mind is the possibility that additional funds may be required in the case of medical requirements for your pet or changed circumstances of the caretaker.

Unlike a will, pet trusts are valid during the pet owner's life as well as after his or her death, and therefore can become effective if you become incapacitated and are unable to care for your pet. In addition, you have complete control over how the funds will be disbursed, although too specific instructions may backfire and become overly inflexible in the case of changed circumstances. Finally, pet trust funds and money earned by the trust from the use of those funds will not be part of your estate and therefore not subject to estate tax at the time of your death.

It is a good idea to distribute copies of all pet trust documents to everyone who signed them, as well as those who are only mentioned in them.

Pet Guardian Options

If you are not able to find a person both willing and able to take care of your pet after you die, you are not without options. Programs exist across the United States that allow you to leave your pet to a trustworthy caretaker after you die.

For example, a growing number of for-profit and not-for-profit pet guardian programs have become popular, including shelters or re-homing organizations. Some are run by university veterinary schools or are associated with local humane societies. Remember, you can put an animal care organization in charge of your pet's care, while naming a separate trustee to oversee the funds and disbursements of the trust.

Legal Owner of a Pet

Keep in mind that whatever estate planning option you choose to provide for your pet, it is important to establish who your pet's legal owner is. Otherwise, all your planning could go to waste.

CHAPTER 11

Estate Taxes

Estate Taxes

When accountants, lawyers and others who deal with these matters refer to "estate tax" they are usually referring to federal tax, not state tax. This distinction is made for three main reasons: (i) many states do not impose an inheritance or death tax; (ii) federal tax is likely to devour more of an estate than state tax will; and (iii) reducing the federal estate tax will often result in a reduction of state taxes as well.

Federal Estate and Gift Tax

The U.S. tax system generally taxes transfers of wealth. This means the federal government usually charges a tax when money or other assets are transferred from one person to another. Keeping this general rule in mind helps to understand estate and gift taxes.

Gift tax, unlike most income taxes, is assessed on the giver and not the receiver. As such, if you make a gift of cash or other property to someone, you will be assessed a gift tax unless you fall within the scope of the exceptions set out under the headings below. When gift tax is payable, you will need to record details of the gift on IRS Form 709. Like many other tax forms, the gift tax form is generally due on April 15th in the year following the calendar year in which you made the gift.

Similarly, when you die another transfer of assets takes place from you to someone else. In this case, an estate tax is imposed on the giver (i.e. your estate). A federal estate tax return is reported on IRS form 706 and needs to be filed with the IRS within nine months of the date of your death unless an extension is obtained.

Everyone's "Coupon"

For purposes of your personal tax and estate planning, gifts made during your lifetime and the value of your estate passed along to your beneficiaries at the time of your death should be considered together. The reason is that under federal tax law, each individual has what is called an "exclusion amount," which is a combined value of gifts during your lifetime and estate assets at death that are excluded from gift and estate taxes.

Simply speaking, the maximum amount you can transfer without incurring gift or estate taxes is like a "coupon." When the total value of your gifts and estate are calculated, you can apply this "coupon" to minimize or avoid the tax. You will only have to pay gift or estate tax if your gifts and/ or transfers at death exceed this "coupon" amount.

In 2025, the "coupon" for gifts and estates (i.e. the "exclusion amount") is $13,990,000 . That means that you can transfer up to $13,990,000 in gifts during your lifetime to anyone you choose and there will not be any gift tax due. However, if you exceed the value of the "coupon," you will owe tax on the excess value of the gifts.

For example, if you give $5 million of taxable gifts to each of your three children over your lifetime, you will have made $15 million in taxable gifts. You can use your "coupon" to avoid tax on the first $13,990,000 but you will owe tax on the other $1,010,000 .

How does this relate to estate taxes? Well, the "coupon" you have available as an exclusion from estate taxes is equal to the exclusion amount in the year that you die less the amount you have given away in gifts during your lifetime.

Returning to the previous example, let's say you made those three $5 million gifts to your children and still had $2 million in your taxable estate when you died in 2025, when the estate tax "coupon" is $13,990,000 . Because you used the full $13,990,000 gift tax "coupon" during your lifetime, your estate tax "coupon" is reduced by $13,990,000 to $0, and estate tax will be owed on the entire $2 million value of your estate.

Example of Coupon

Anna gave James and John a total of $10 million during her lifetime that used up most of her lifetime gifting exemption of $13,990,000 . Anna died in 2025. The estate tax threshold in 2025 was $13,990,000. However, to determine whether Anna had reached her estate tax exemption threshold, the gifts she made during her lifetime will be taken into account. As such, on her death, her exemption would only be $3,990,000 ($13,990,000 less the $10 million gift tax exemption used).

How to Determine the Estate Tax?

The first question to ask when trying to determine the amount of federal estate tax which might be due by your estate is, "What is the fair market value of everything you own, control, or have an interest in at the date of your death?" In answering this question, you will need to include all the assets you own, such as cash, investments, real estate, cars, boats, art, and the like. Estate tax is also levied on the life insurance policies in your name where you have a right of ownership in the policy.

The total value of all these items is called your "gross estate." Your "taxable estate" is your gross estate less certain deductions. These deductions may include mortgages on your assets, debts you owe, estate administration expenses, property that passes automatically to your surviving spouse on your death, and bequests to qualified charities (more on the deductions for spouses and charities below).

Once you have calculated your taxable estate, estate tax may be owed if the value of the taxable estate exceeds the unused portion of your estate tax "coupon."

Just as the value of the "coupon" changes depending on the year in which you make a gift or die, the percentage of the tax assessment also changes.

Year of Gift/Death	Maximum Gift Tax	Maximum Estate Tax
2009	45%	45%
2010	35%	N/A
2011 & 2012	35%	35%
2013 to 2025	40%	40%

State Taxes

Not every state imposes a separate state tax on estates or inheritances. Florida, for instance, imposes no state death tax. Where there is such a tax, it is likely to be one (or a combination) of three types of tax: (1) death tax, (2) inheritance tax, or (3) pick-up tax.

State Death Taxes

When people use the phrase "death tax," they are generally referring to taxes levied by the state on a deceased person's estate upon death. The amount of state tax due, if any, is determined on a state-by-state basis according to that state's tax laws and is often calculated in a manner like federal estate tax.

State Inheritance Taxes

In states with inheritance tax laws, inheritance tax is usually paid by the person who receives assets either under a will or through intestacy. In some states, the tax is levied on the estate itself so that the tax must be paid by the estate before calculating what can be distributed to beneficiaries. One tax rate may apply to all assets in the estate, or the rate may vary depending upon who receives what property. Generally, the closer the person receiving a gift from the deceased is to the deceased (in terms of blood line), the lower the tax rate on the transfer of property to that person. Thus, depending on what class the beneficiary falls into, he or she will be taxed at a specific rate.

States with Inheritance Taxes or Estate Taxes			
State	**Tax Collected**	**State**	**Tax Collected**
Connecticut	Estate Tax	Nebraska	Inheritance Tax
Delaware	Estate Tax, expires on July 1, 2013	New Jersey	Estate Tax and Inheritance Tax
District of Columbia	Estate Tax	New York	Estate Tax
Hawaii	Estate Tax	North Carolina	Estate Tax
Illinois	Estate Tax	Oregon	Estate Tax
Iowa	Inheritance Tax	Pennsylvania	Inheritance Tax
Kentucky	Inheritance Tax	Rhode Island	Estate Tax
Maine	Estate Tax	Tennessee	Estate Tax
Maryland	Estate Tax & Inheritance Tax	Vermont	Estate Tax
Massachusetts	Estate Tax	Washington	Estate Tax
Minnesota	Estate Tax		

State 'Pick-Up' Taxes

Some states determine all, or a portion of their state death tax based on the amount of federal estate tax credit allowed against payments of state death taxes. Prior to 2001, federal estate taxes could be reduced by a credit for state death taxes paid on an estate. The result was that the federal estate tax was a "maximum" tax that was paid partly to the state and partly to the federal government. Many states therefore would "pick-up" their tax revenue by pegging their state death taxes at the amount of the federal credit that you could claim for state death taxes. After 2001, the federal government gradually eliminated the credit for state death taxes. However, some states chose to continue to charge a pick-up tax based on what the federal credit was in 2001, even though the federal credit is no longer available.

For all three of the types of tax a state might assess, some states will have a "coupon" equal to the federal tax "coupon," meaning that if there is no federal estate tax there is no state estate tax. However, many states have chosen not to increase their "coupons" at the same rate that the federal law does, so the state "coupon" may be smaller, resulting in state estate tax being payable even where federal estate tax is not payable.

Marital Deduction

Remember the gift and estate tax "coupon" for federal taxes? Historically, it was unique to each individual/estate and could not be used by anyone else. That meant that you had a "coupon", and your spouse had a "coupon," and they were non-transferable.

The "coupons" are not used up by gifts made or estates transferred to a spouse who is a U.S. citizen. Instead, federal gift/estate tax applies an unlimited deduction to those transfers. In other words, you can gift or transfer an unlimited amount of property to your U.S. citizen spouse and there is no gift or estate tax on that transfer.

That is the good news. The bad news is that the marital deduction is, in some ways, just a waiting game whereby the government allows you to transfer your property on a tax-free basis to your spouse with the view that it will later be taxed when your spouse dies or gives it away. As your spouse could not use your gift/estate tax "coupon" prior to the introduction of the Tax Relief, Unemployment Insurance Reauthorization, and Job Creation Act of 2010, in December 2010, that meant that your spouse had more to transfer to her beneficiaries and heirs but without the benefit of an increased the "coupon". However, in December 2010, President Obama signed this legislation into law which entitled a person to use any unused element of his or her deceased spouse's coupon. However, that right could be lost if the surviving spouse remarried and his/her new spouse predeceased him/her.

Consider this example: Your last will & testament provides for your spouse to inherit everything you own when you die. At your death, your net taxable estate is $15 million, and your spouse also has an estate worth $15 million. Since your spouse was the recipient of your estate, the unlimited marital deduction applies and there is no estate tax due because of your death regardless of the applicable "coupon". If your spouse dies in 2025, under current law your spouse's maximum "coupon" will be $27,980,000 ($13,990,000 of his or her own plus $13,990,000 of yours) assuming neither of you previously used any element of your coupon. Of course, to the extent that either of you used your coupon, this amount will be deducted from the $24,120,000 coupon. Ultimately, your spouse's estate will be subject to tax on the excess of "$2,020,000 ($30,000,0000 - $27,980,000). At a tax rate of 40%, that translates to a tax of $808,000.

To take advantage of the portability rule, the executor handling the estate of the spouse who died must elect to transfer the unused exclusion to the survivor, who can then use it to make lifetime gifts or pass assets through his or her estate. In order to do so, the executor must file an estate tax return when the first spouse dies—even if no tax is owed—within nine months after the first spouse's death and make the portability election on that tax return. If the executor misses this deadline, the surviving spouse loses the right to portability.

Important Note

A surviving spouse may lose the right to use his or her deceased spouse's coupon if he or she remarries.

Non-Citizen Spouses

The unlimited marital deduction is available only when you give or leave your assets to a spouse who is a U.S. citizen at the time the transfer is made. Some types of credit shelter trust planning mechanisms are also only effective if your spouse is a U.S. citizen. If your spouse is not a citizen, your estate plan must include more sophisticated trust planning designed to keep the assets in the United States managed by a U.S. trustee so that the trust can qualify for the marital deduction that is otherwise only available to U.S. citizen spouses. This is called a Qualified Domestic Trust ("QDOT"). For more information, speak to your attorney.

Charitable Deductions

You probably already know that you get an income tax deduction when you donate to a charity during your lifetime. You can also save on estate taxes by giving to charity. Any bequest you make from your estate to a qualified charity is exempt from federal estate tax. You can also combine estate tax planning and income tax planning by setting up a trust with a charity as one of the beneficiaries.

Charitable Remainder Trust

The most common charitable trust is a charitable remainder trust ("CRT"). With this type of trust, you donate an asset or assets to the trust during your lifetime. You can continue to get some income from the trust assets, but the charity gets the remainder of what is in the trust when you die or when the term of the trust otherwise ends. Because you have donated to the trust, you will be allowed to take an income tax deduction equal to the estimated value of the charity's remainder. You have also removed the asset in the trust from your estate, so it will not be subject to estate taxes when you die. Yet you can still enjoy a regular payout from the trust assets. The amount of income you get from the trust may be either a fixed percentage of the assets you donated to the trust or a percentage of the trust's value each year. Of course, if you choose to peg your payment on the value of the trust, your payment will fluctuate as the value of the assets in the trust fluctuates.

Some CRTs are especially attractive if you have assets that have appreciated in value. By placing the asset into the trust, you may be able to minimize the capital gains taxes you would otherwise have had to pay when you sold the asset.

Let us look at how a CRT would work in an example. Anna and David are a retired couple who own vacant land that they purchased many years ago and which is not producing any income for them. The value of the land has gone up considerably, so they would have to pay significant capital gains tax if they sold it. Rather than sell the land, pay the capital gains tax, and then invest the after-tax proceeds to produce income, they decide to create a CRT and donate the land to the trust. Once the land has been transferred to the trust, the trust is free to sell the land without having to pay any capital gains tax on the sale. The CRT can then use the proceeds of the sale to provide an income to Anna and David for as long either of them is alive. After they both die, the remainder of the trust assets can be given to a charity of their choosing.

In addition, after establishing the CRT and transferring the land to it, Anna and David can take an immediate income tax deduction for the estimated value of the amount that the trust will give to their chosen charity. They may have to pay some tax on the income they receive from the trust, but probably not as much as they would have had to pay upfront if they had just sold the land (this should be determined in the planning stage). Furthermore, the value of the land is no longer in their estates, so there will not be any estate tax assessed on that value.

Charitable Remainder Trust

```
                                    Annual
                                   Payment
            Land                    to You

                    ▲
                    │
            ┌───────────────────────────────┐
            │  Charitable Remainder Trust   │
            └───────────────────────────────┘

                    Assets left in Trust
                      go to Charity
```

Charitable Lead Trust

Another type of charitable trust is a charitable lead trust ("CLT"). With a CLT, you transfer property to a trust that then pays an annual income, called "the lead," to a charity. When the trust terminates after a specified number of years, the remaining assets left in the trust go to a person or persons you name, such as your children. Generally, you won't get an income tax deduction for giving any property to a CLT, but you won't pay any gift tax and you have removed some of the value of the asset from your estate. A CLT can be a good choice for an asset that is expected to appreciate in the future, so that the appreciated value will not be in your estate.

Returning to our previous example, assume that Anna and David have another piece of land that they expect to be worth much more in the coming years as the area around the land is developed, and which they believe they can lease to generate some annual income. They decide to establish a charitable lead trust that in five years will begin to pay a percentage of the annual trust income to their favorite charity. When the trust is terminated in fifteen years, the assets remaining in the trust will go to their grandchildren. There may be a taxable gift to the grandchildren depending on the estimated value of the gift that passes to them, but that estimated value will be based on the value of the land now, and will not include the high appreciation expected in the near future. Anna and David have removed the value of the asset from their estate, provided for their favorite charity, and assured that the land as it appreciates will benefit their grandchildren in the future.

For more information on CLTs, speak to your attorney or tax advisor.

Charitable Lead Trust

Land

Annual Payment to Charity

Charitable Lead Trust

When Trust ends, Assets go to Beneficiaries

Other Ways to Reduce Estate Taxes

Federal estate tax can be reduced through a variety of other legitimate estate planning techniques. Although the increase of the "coupon" to $13,990,000 per person has set a high threshold before estates are taxed, those with estates valued at greater than this amount could benefit from some of the methods of reducing potential estate tax liability that we discuss below. The advantages and disadvantages of these techniques vary greatly depending on the individual circumstances of the persons using them, and therefore this is one area where having an experienced attorney or tax advisor can be beneficial.

Lifetime Gifts

A gift made to a spouse who is a U.S. citizen is not taxed, regardless of the value of the gift. Gifts made to noncitizen spouses are tax free up to $190,000 for 2025.

Under federal tax law, gifts of less than a specified amount each year incur no gift tax, do not require filing of a gift tax return, and do not even use up any of your "coupon." The excluded amount is pegged to inflation, so it will vary each year. For example, in 2025 you can make a tax-exempt gift to any individual provided the total amount of gifts to that person during the calendar year does not exceed $19,000. This exemption applies to each person making a gift, which means that if both you and your spouse utilize this estate planning tool, you could collectively reduce your estate by giving away $36,000 a year to each of any number of beneficiaries, free of any federal gift tax. Over a period of several years, the amount of money that you and your spouse (or partner) could transfer to your intended beneficiaries under this method could be quite substantial.

You can also make tax-free gifts by paying someone's medical expenses or tuition bills, provided you pay the bill directly to the medical or educational institution. Gifts of this type are not subject to the annual exemption limits and can be in any amount.

Making lifetime gifts as described above removes the gifted assets from your estate, potentially reducing the amount your estate would otherwise have to pay in federal estate tax. You must plan carefully, however, because in some cases the effect of capital gains taxes could make lifetime gifts less advantageous than inheritances at the time of your death.

Capital gain is the amount you receive when you sell an asset minus your "basis" in that asset. Broadly speaking, basis is the amount you have invested in the asset. So, if you sell an asset for $100 and your basis in that asset is $10, you will have a capital gain of $90 that is subject to capital gains tax. When you make a gift during your lifetime, the recipient of the gift will have the same basis in the gifted asset as you had at the time the gift was made—this is referred to as a "carry-over basis." Therefore, if you gift the asset with a $10 basis and the recipient sells it for $100, the recipient will have the same $90 capital gain that you would have had if you had sold the asset yourself. In contrast, if you leave that same asset as an inheritance rather than a lifetime gift, your recipient now gets a "stepped up basis" to the value of the asset on the date that you died. So, if the value of the asset was $100 when you died, the recipient would now have a basis of $100 (rather than a carry-over basis of $10). If the recipient then sells the asset for $100, there will be no capital gains subject to tax. Therefore, transferring the asset at the time of your death produces significant tax savings for the recipient. In our example, since capital gains taxes are currently around 15 percent, gifting the asset would have cost the recipient $13.50 in capital gains tax (15 percent of $90), while inheriting the asset wouldn't have cost the recipient any tax. This difference in basis is why it is important to consult a tax advisor before making significant lifetime gifts as part of your estate planning.

Let us consider another example: Adam dies in 2025 leaving all his property to his three children. His entire estate consists of nine apartment houses, each worth $1 million dollars. Adam's original basis in each apartment house was $200,000, or a total of $1.8 million in original basis for the total estate. Upon Adam's death, however, his children will receive apartment houses with a stepped-up basis of $1 million each. Therefore, if Adam's estate sells all the apartment houses for $1 million each before distributing the proceeds to Adam's children, those sales would result in no capital gains tax.

If Adam's estate does not sell all the apartment houses, but instead transfers three of them to each of his three children, each child would receive 3 apartment houses each with a basis of $1 million. The children would not have to pay capital gains tax when the inheritance is received, but if any apartment house appreciated in value before it was sold, the child holding that apartment building would have to pay capital gains tax on the difference between the appreciated value and the $1 million basis.

Based on the relative complexity of these examples, you can see the benefit of getting tax advice in this area of estate planning.

Note: This example assumes that each apartment house has the same original basis. If the original basis is different for each asset, the new basis will also be different for each asset, as the new basis is the proportional share of stepped up basis plus the original basis.

Irrevocable Life Insurance Trusts

An irrevocable life insurance trust creates a trust that is used exclusively to own life insurance. The trust purchases life insurance on your life, and you make gifts to the trust to pay the premiums. The trust may not be revoked and once you place funds into the trust, they cannot be taken back. Upon your death, the life insurance payout to your trust is distributed according to the terms of the trust. Because you do not control the life insurance, it is not considered part of your taxable estate and thus no federal estate taxes are due when the payout is made.

Family Limited Partnerships

A family limited partnership ("FLP") is created to hold and manage family assets. Once the limited partnership is created, you transfer whatever assets you determine to the FLP in exchange for an interest in the partnership. Subsequently, you can gift all or a portion of your partnership interest to your children, perhaps over several years. Often, an FLP is used to help a family transfer ownership of its closely held businesses to the next generation of business managers.

FLPs can save estate taxes in two ways. First, they can remove from your estate assets that are likely to appreciate, potentially saving estate taxes at the time of your death. And even though the asset is removed from the estate, you may retain control over the partnership and therefore continue to have control over how the asset is managed. Second, any gift you make to your children of a percentage interest in an FLP may be valued at less than the same percentage value of the underlying assets in the partnership.

For example, assume you establish an FLP with three pieces of real estate each valued at $500,000, so the value of the assets in the FLP totals $1,500,000. Afterwards, you gift a ten percent interest in the partnership to your son. While ten percent of the value of the partnership assets is $150,000 ($1,500,000 x .10), the fair market value of a ten percent interest in the partnership may be appreciably less than $150,000. This is because as a ten percent owner, your son doesn't have control over the assets and it is not likely that he can find someone willing to pay him $150,000 for the chance to be a minority partner without any partnership control. The actual fair market value of the ten percent partnership interest depends on many factors, which is why you must be prepared to get a qualified appraisal on the gift when you use an FLP as part of your estate plan. For more information, speak to your attorney or tax advisor.

Special Use Real Estate Valuation

Generally, real estate you transfer by way of a gift or on your death is valued based on the assumption that the real estate will be sold for its "highest and best use" value. For example, farmland may be worth much more if it was sold for residential development than for agricultural use. However, you or your estate may be able to claim that the real estate should be valued based on its "actual use" value rather than the "highest and best use" value. This can result in significant tax savings, especially if your family intends to continue using the land as farmland rather than selling it to a developer. Special use valuation is complicated and generally requires the assistance of an experienced attorney and valuation agent.

Conclusion

Estate taxes and estate tax planning are a complicated area of the law. If you have an estate greater than a million dollars or have other special circumstances, we recommend that you seek professional advice before employing any of the tax reduction strategies referred to in this chapter.

CHAPTER 12

Same-Sex Married Couples, Unmarried Couples, and Divorced Couples

Same-Sex Married Couples

Until recently, same-sex couples who were legally married were unable to take advantage of the rights, privileges and benefits contained in the more than 1,000 federal statutes and regulations that apply to married spouses. This was because Section 3 of the Defense of Marriage Act ("DOMA"), enacted in 1996, defined the word "marriage" in any federal law or regulation to mean only "a legal union between one man and one woman as husband and wife." In addition, DOMA defined "spouse" as a "person of the opposite sex who is a husband and wife." This meant that married same-sex spouses were unable to file joint tax returns, take advantage of the marital exemption for gifts and inheritances, etc. In other words, DOMA had a huge financial impact on these legally married couples.

However, a vast section of the regulatory landscape for same-sex married couples changed on June 26, 2013, when the U.S. Supreme Court ruled in United States v. Windsor that Section 3 of DOMA violated the equal protection clause of the Fifth Amendment to the U.S. Constitution. As a result, for federal purposes, same-sex couples who are legally married must now be treated the same as opposite-sex married couples—at least to the extent they reside in a jurisdiction that allows marriage between same-sex couples.

Future Supreme Court intervention in the form of Obergefell v. Hodges in 2015 resulted in the recognition of same-sex marriage in all 50 states.

An important question that the Supreme Court did not answer in Windsor was whether the decision applied to a couple who were married in a state that allows same-sex marriage and then moved to a state that does not. However, on August 29, 2013, The U.S. Internal Revenue Service ("IRS") issued Revenue Ruling 2013-17, stating that all legally married same-sex couples—including those couples residing in states that don't recognize same-sex marriage—will be recognized as married for federal tax purposes.

It should be noted that Revenue Ruling 2013-17 does not cover federal benefits administered by other federal agencies. However, certain other agencies have already announced that they will recognize same-sex marriages that were valid in the place where the marriage was performed.

Estate Planning After the Supreme Court Decisions

Following the Windsor decision, many federal benefits related to estate planning that were previously unavailable to married same-sex couples have now become available. As a result, it has become imperative that married same-sex couples who already had an estate plan that was devised to maximize benefits for an unmarried couple (See the section on "Unmarried Couples" below) now review and revise that plan to take advantage of the opportunities afforded by changes in the law.

For example, you should review your will, revocable trusts, retirement account and life insurance beneficiary designations, and title to assets to make sure you have an optimum plan to take advantage of previously unavailable benefits. And if you did not have an estate plan previously, the Supreme Court rulings give you a huge incentive to create one.

Federal benefits related to estate planning that are now available to married same-sex couples include:

- The Marital Deduction
- Portability
- Gift Splitting
- Retirement Plan Beneficiary Designations
- Rollover Rights
- Social Security Survivor's Benefits
- Joint Income Tax Return

The Marital Deduction

This extremely important deduction allows spouses to transfer an unlimited amount of assets to each other, either by gift during their lifetime or by inheritance at the time of death, without having to pay any federal estate or gift tax (provided that the recipient is a U.S. citizen). This means that when the first spouse dies, no estate taxes are incurred on any cash or property inherited by the surviving spouse.

Portability

As described in Chapter 11, "portability" is the right of a surviving spouse to add the unused tax 'coupon' of the deceased spouse to his or her own available coupon. To take advantage of portability, the executor of the deceased spouse transfers the unused tax coupon to the surviving spouse, who can then use it to make lifetime gifts or pass assets at death up to the combined amount of the two coupon credits on a tax-free basis.

Gift-splitting

Under federal law, an individual can currently give up to $19,000 annually to as many individuals as he or she would like without incurring any gift tax. But spouses can combine this amount and jointly give $36,000 to any person without tax. This amount can come from each of their accounts, one individual's account, or a joint account.

In addition, any gift—or aggregate gifts—to an individual that has a greater value than the annual exclusion amount counts against the lifetime gift tax exclusion amount (which is currently $13,990,000). Once an individual has exceeded the lifetime gift tax exclusion amount, any further gifts may be subject to gift tax. But married couples can also gift-split with their lifetime exclusion amount, so together they can transfer up to $27,980,000 in gifts during their lifetimes without any gift tax.

Right to be Named the Beneficiary on Company Retirement Plans

If one spouse participates in a "qualified plan" plan under the Employee Retirement Income Security Act of 1974 ("ERISA")—which includes defined-contribution plans, defined benefit plans, and 401(k) plans—then the other spouse has the right to be the sole primary beneficiary of the account. To name another person as beneficiary requires the second spouse's written consent.

Rollover Rights

For ERISA-qualified plans and IRAs (which are not "qualified plans"), the law gives special privileges to spouses who inherit the funds. Beneficiaries who are not spouses must begin making withdrawals by December 31 of the year following the account owner's death. However, a surviving spouse who inherits funds in an ERISA-qualified plan or IRA account can roll the assets into his or her own IRA and postpone the required minimum withdrawals until the year after the surviving spouse turns 70 ½ years old.

Social Security Survivor's Benefits

When one spouse dies, the surviving spouse may be eligible for Social Security survivor's benefits if the surviving spouse is 60 years of age or older, 50 years of age or older and disabled, or any age if he or she is caring for the decedent's child who is younger than 16 years of age and entitled to Social Security benefits based on the deceased individual's contributions.

Joint Income Tax Return

Married spouses can file joint income tax returns, which in most cases results in a lower combined tax than the total amount the two persons would have paid by filing as single persons.

Retroactive Benefits

A statute that is ruled unconstitutional is considered void from the beginning. Therefore, given the Windsor decision, same-sex married couples should always have been treated the same as opposite-sex married couples for purposes of federal law. As a result, some same-sex married couples who would have paid less in federal income and estate taxes had they been permitted to file joint federal income tax returns, claim the marital deduction upon the death of a spouse or upon a lifetime gift to the spouse, etc., may now file amended income tax and estate tax returns (and should do so as soon as possible).

Unmarried Couples—Opposite-Sex and Same-Sex Partners

Estate Planning Options for Unmarried Couples

Of all the specific types of people who face an estate planning challenge to have their intentions honored, unmarried couples—including same-sex unmarried couples—may face the most difficulty.

There are millions of unmarried couples in the United States, and all are at a disadvantage when it comes to financial and estate planning. This is because they are unable to take advantage of the myriad laws and tax advantages that benefit married couples—which at the federal level now includes same-sex married couples. As a result, if you are in a committed relationship but are unmarried, it becomes especially important for you to understand all of the planning options we've laid out in this book and how you can best utilize them. Failure to do so may result in your clear intentions with respect to your partner not being honored at the time of your death or incapacity.

For example, the surviving partner in an unmarried relationship has no right of spousal election under state law to a share of the decedent's estate, and no presumptive right of survivorship to such assets as the primary residence or bank accounts. In addition, unmarried partners are not entitled to the federal marital exclusion for gift and estate tax purposes, portability, or gift-splitting rules. They are also not entitled to receive Social Security survivor's benefits and have no absolute right to be the beneficiary of qualified pension plans. Finally, their ability to act as guardians of minor children who are not their own will also come into serious question.

To prevent unintended results, it is therefore critical for unmarried couples to execute clear and enforceable instructions and documents concerning the management of their finances and healthcare in the event of incapacity, and the disposition of their estate at the time of death. If you do not execute the proper estate planning documents, your partner will likely have no rights in making financial or medical decisions on your behalf and will not inherit from your estate. Further, the default rules in the state where you reside at the time of death will most likely put these decisions in the hands of, and transfer your assets to, individuals who you did not select.

Remember, if you haven't created an estate plan, your state's law of intestacy will apply, and the rules set out under that law will mostly likely require that your assets be transferred in the way that does not match what you would have wanted. State laws vary, but generally they transfer assets to the closest family members. In this case, an unmarried partner will not receive any of your assets.

To avoid this scenario and have your intentions honored as closely as possible, some of the specific estate planning options that unmarried couples should pay particular attention to are:

- Wills
- Revocable Living Trusts
- Titling/Ownership of Property
- Life Insurance
- Beneficiary Designations
- Healthcare and Financial Powers of Attorney

Now we will take a closer look at these estate planning options as they relate to unmarried partners.

Will

The easiest way to leave your partner some or all your assets at death is to create a will that bequeaths all or a portion of your estate to your partner. One disadvantage of a will is that it must go through probate and therefore its contents will be publicly available. Not only does this destroy any privacy regarding what you leave your partner, it also opens these gifts up to a challenge by other persons such as family members. If your partner loses such a challenge, your wishes to transfer assets to him or her may be thwarted. And even if your partner prevails, it will only be after losing a significant amount of time and money in the process of defending the challenge.

Revocable Living Trust

A revocable living trust allows you to avoid some of the potential disadvantages of a will, as well as those of joint ownership and beneficiary designations described below. In fact, if you are in an unmarried relationship, this is probably one of the best ways to ensure your assets are managed by your partner in the event of your incapacity and transferred to your partner at the time of your death.

First, you can appoint your partner as your successor trustee to serve in the event of your incapacitation or death. Then upon your death, your partner as successor trustee distributes the assets as provided for in the trust agreement without going through probate and without providing public notice. This assures that the transfer of assets to your partner will be quick and confidential, as well as difficult to challenge. And the trust is revocable, so if you separate from your partner before you die, you can easily cancel the trust or change its terms.

Titling/Ownership of Property

One of the best forms of ownership for unmarried couples is as joint tenants with right of survivorship ("JTWROS"). With JTWROS, when one of the owners dies, the property automatically transfers to the surviving owner outside of probate.

However, transferring a deed to a partner in JTWROS is an irrevocable decision which can create unintended consequences. For example, these assets become exposed to your partner's creditors, and your partner will have access to the assets and may not take good care of them. In addition, there are gift tax, income tax and estate tax issues which should be thoroughly understood before choosing this option.

Another option available to unmarried couples is tenants in common. Under this ownership option, when one partner dies his or her percentage ownership becomes part of their estate. If there is a will in place the property will pass to the heirs listed in the will, but this brings into play the disadvantages of a will that we just discussed. As a result, this is not perhaps the best option for unmarried couples.

Beneficiary Designations on Retirement Accounts

Most rules governing the designation of beneficiaries on retirement accounts do not contemplate an unmarried partner unless one is specifically named as beneficiary. Therefore, if you would like your partner to inherit retirement account assets which go to a beneficiary on your death, you must carefully review the documents pertaining to these assets and make sure you have named your partner as the beneficiary in the proper manner. A beneficiary designation takes precedence over any will and the assets pass outside of probate. Keep in mind that for ERISA-qualified plans and IRAs, your unmarried partner will probably not be able to roll-over these assets into their own IRA.

Life Insurance

Life insurance is one of the best ways to protect your unmarried partner. He or she can receive substantial amounts of cash outside of probate when you die, and these funds can be used to make up for the loss of joint income due to your death, as well as to pay any taxes they incur by inheriting other assets. Keep in mind that some insurance carriers make it difficult for unmarried partners to designate each other as beneficiaries of life insurance, so you may have to search for a carrier willing to do so on acceptable terms.

Irrevocable Life Insurance Trust

If you have a larger estate, you may also want to consider an irrevocable life insurance trust under which the proceeds paid to the trust on your death will not be included in your gross estate for tax purposes. The lack of a marital deduction makes it more likely that an unmarried couple will want to utilize this vehicle than a married couple.

Financial Power of Attorney

For unmarried couples wishing to give each other the right to manage their partner's affairs in the event of their incapacity, a durable general power of attorney is critical. If you fail to execute a durable general power of attorney and later become incapacitated or otherwise unable to make your own decisions and manage your own financial affairs, then a court will appoint a guardian or conservator to do so, and that person is unlikely to be your partner.

Healthcare Power of Attorney and Living Will

For the same reasons, if you want your partner to make your healthcare decisions in the event of your incapacity, then it is vital that you create a healthcare power of attorney and living will naming your partner as the person to make those decisions for you. You should also stipulate that your partner has visitation rights and the ability to obtain access to your medical records. Keep in mind that in the absence of your ability to make your own choices, state law normally provides for an order of priority in selecting who will make these types of decisions—and this hierarchy does not include an unmarried partner.

Funeral Arrangements

The laws of some states allow you to designate, in a signed and notarized writing, your partner as the person to plan for your funeral and the disposition of your remains.

Guardianship

If you and your partner have minor children together, you can use your will to name a guardian for these children if both partners die. If you have a minor child and your partner is not the parent, then you may want to take additional precautions if you want your partner to continue to be involved in your child's life after you pass away, because his or her guardianship may be challenged. For example, you can name your partner as successor trustee for any trust that you create with your child as a beneficiary.

Civil Unions and Domestic Partnerships

For same-sex unmarried couples, many states offer domestic partnerships, civil unions, or similar methods of legal recognition that confer some or all the state rights, duties, and liabilities as a legally married spouse. If you are in a same-sex unmarried relationship and reside in such a state, you should explore this option as part of your estate planning.

Divorced Couples

Revising Your Estate Plan Following Divorce

The reality of modern society is that many people get divorced. And from an estate planning standpoint, divorce changes the entire equation, especially if a plan is already in place. So if you anticipate getting divorced or have already gotten divorced, you should review and revise your estate plan to literally unhitch yourself from your previous spouse and create a plan that best suits an unmarried individual. It is even more crucial that you do this if you are, or anticipate getting, remarried.

The estate planning areas and documents that you should review in preparation for divorce include your:

- Will
- Living Trusts
- Beneficiary Designations
- Healthcare and Financial Powers of Attorney
- Living Will

For example, if you created a will and other estate planning documents when you were married, you probably left most of your assets to your spouse and named him or her as the decision-maker for your financial and healthcare decisions in the event you became incapacitated. But divorced couples (and even those in the process of getting divorced) normally no longer want their former spouse to inherit their estate or the assets of a revocable living trust, let alone be granted a power of attorney or be the designated decision-maker in an advance directive.

Creating a New Will

If your former spouse is named as a beneficiary in your will, the easiest and surest way to remove that person is to create a new will that includes a revocation clause specifying that the previous will is revoked, and destroy all copies of the old one for good measure. This guarantees that he or she will not inherit any assets under your will. If you do not do this and your former spouse remains in your will, it will depend on the law or your state of residence at death as to whether they still inherit under the will. Some states automatically invalidate provisions in wills for ex-spouses; others allow them to inherit as stated in the will.

This issue becomes even more complicated if you remarry. Although spousal election laws protect new spouses who were not named in a will created before marriage, collecting in this manner will probably involve considerable time and expense.

If you have minor children, you may also need to adjust your new will that take into account your divorce. If you leave money or property to your children, you may not want your ex-spouse to have access to that money. If this is the case, you should create a trust for your minor children and name a trustee who is not your ex-spouse, and provide instructions that insure the money will not pass through his or her possession. For example, you can instruct that the trustee only use the funds for specific purposes that benefit the child, and can state that the funds must be paid directly to certain designated institutions, such as schools or hospitals, rather than to the child's guardian directly.

In a related matter, you should name a guardian in your will to care for your children in the event both you and your ex-spouse die or become incapacitated, or your ex-spouse does not want to care for the children.

Finally, you need to decide who will be the executor of your new will. Be careful with this decision, especially if you have children. If you name someone whose duty as executor may cause friction among your children, etc., you may want to make a different choice.

Revoking or Revising Your Trusts

Trusts are one of the best and most common means for married partners to transfer assets at the time of death outside of probate, especially to children. Once you divorce, however, you will most likely want to revoke or change the terms of any trust you have set up.

If the trust is a revocable living trust providing "first for your spouse and then for your children," then this provision may remain in place after your divorce unless you revoke or amend the trust document. Fortunately, if the trust is revocable, then you can amend the trust to include agreed upon terms, or you can dissolve the trust and remove its assets—which will then be included in the marital assets at the time of divorce.

With respect to your minor children, you will probably want to follow the same course recommended in the section on "Creating a New Will" above. Similarly, you will need to take the same care in naming a successor trustee as you would in naming an executor of your will.

Creating New Powers of Attorney and Living Wills

Normally, following a divorce you will not want your ex-spouse to make healthcare or financial decisions on your behalf. Therefore, once you have decided to get a divorce it is important to execute new general durable powers of attorney, healthcare durable powers of attorney, and living wills. You should also revoke and destroy the old documents, as well as provide copies of the new documents to the relevant persons so they know your intent.

Property Ownership

If you co-own property with your spouse that will not be assigned to one party or the other as part of the divorce settlement, you may want to sever the joint tenancy and share the property as "tenants in common," which can pass on death to a beneficiary you name in your new will rather than to your surviving ex-spouse as joint tenant.

Beneficiary Designations

You undoubtedly have some assets that pass directly to a named beneficiary and do not go through probate at the time of your death, and it is likely that your former spouse was named as the beneficiary of these assets. If you do not want these assets to go to your ex-spouse when you die, then you need to properly change the beneficiary designation on all relevant plans and accounts, including life insurance, retirement plans, IRAs, bank accounts with "pay-on-death" designations, etc.

Although like wills, some such designations may be automatically revoked upon divorce, you should not rely on this. If you fail to change these designations and they are not revoked by law or contract, your former spouse who was the original designated beneficiary will be entitled to the benefit. Keep in mind that if you are not yet divorced, your spouse may have to sign a written waiver permitting you to change beneficiaries on certain accounts such as ERISA-qualified plans.

In addition, as mentioned above you should take care in naming your replacement beneficiary designations, because if you name your children directly, rather than a trust set up for the benefit of your children, your ex-spouse may have access to the funds.

Divorced Parents

Divorced individuals with minor children must pay close attention to the related issues of guardianship and inheritance. If possible, it is a good idea to speak with your former spouse and agree on a plan for guardianship in the event both of you die and/or become incapacitated.

With respect to inheritance, you need to decide what assets your children will receive from your estate after you die and determine the most appropriate way for them to receive those assets. Typically, the parent will appoint the guardian to manage any funds left to the child. But in the case of divorce, if you are concerned that your child's guardian—probably your ex-spouse—will use the funds inappropriately, consider setting up a revocable living trust to hold and distribute your child's inheritance until they are of age to take possession of the remaining funds.

Separation

If you are contemplating a divorce, then you may want to revise your estate plan as recommended in this section even before your divorce becomes final. Remember that most states provide a surviving spouse with a statutory right of election, so if you die before the divorce is final your spouse will be able to inherit from your estate. In addition, provisions in your will and trusts—as well as beneficiary designations—that benefit your intended-to-be former spouse will still be enforceable.

Estate Planning Upon Subsequent Marriages

If you remarry following a divorce or death of a spouse and you have children from the first marriage, you should pay close attention to how your estate plan treats your children from your first marriage. It is recommended that you create a trust on their behalf if you want them to inherit assets from you. Otherwise, it may end up that your children from your first marriage would receive nothing from your estate, as the estate would pass first to your second spouse if he or she survives you, and then to your second spouses beneficiaries at the time of his or her death.

CHAPTER 13

The Family Business

Creating a Business Estate Plan

If you are a business owner, then your business probably entails a significant portion of your assets. So the success of your estate plan is dependent upon one of the following taking place: the business being successfully transitioned to family member owners and/or managers; the business being sold at or above its fair market value; or the business being managed so that its earnings are maximized, efficiently distributed to you, and then passed along to your beneficiaries at the time of your death.

To accomplish this, you need to take a close look at where the real value of your business lies and how best to maximize that value as part of your estate. If the value of the business is as an ongoing entity in the future, and you have members of your family that are fully capable of acting as owners and/or managers of the business once you are gone, then you can plan for such person or persons to succeed you upon your death, or at an appropriate earlier time.

If this is not the case, then you need to assess whether you would create more value by reinvesting profits in the business and positioning it to be sold at the highest possible price, or taking profits out of the business and investing them elsewhere. This may depend in large part on how critical you are personally to the enterprise—if your business is dependent on you and would significantly decrease in value if you were not around to operate it, then it makes sense to do the latter.

In any event, you need a clearly defined business estate plan, because without one, your unexpected death or incapacitation could throw your business into chaos and cause it to lose most of the value you want to pass along to your chosen beneficiaries. It could even result in your life's work being sold at fire sale prices simply to pay the government the estate tax you owe at the time of your death. Or it could mean control of the business getting tied up in probate for a length of time that could be devastating to its operations and earnings.

To avoid these types of negative results, you need to take the following business estate planning steps:

- Choose the best way to maximize your business assets that will be passed to your heirs—i.e. succession, sale of the company, or distribution of earnings
- Create a succession plan to smoothly transition the business (if the business will continue operations following your death or incapacity)
- Create an estate plan to efficiently pass along the business to its new owners and minimize taxes
- Make provisions in the case of multiple owners

Creating a Succession Plan

If you desire to have your business continue following your death, or to have it operate smoothly in the event of your incapacity or until it can be sold at a fair price, then you need to have a thoroughly developed and clearly communicated succession plan in place. This is not only for the benefit of your heirs, but also for the employees, customers, and others who have helped you build a successful business.

Any comprehensive succession plan entails:

- Choosing who will be the successor owner (or owners) of the business
- Choosing who will be the successor manager of the business
- Setting a time frame for the transition
- Preparing the new owners and managers of the business to take over the business
- Communicating your succession plan clearly to the appropriate persons within the business, as well as to investors, suppliers, key customers, etc.
- Effecting a smooth transition to the new owner/management team

The first thing to decide is what person or person's you want to share in the future profits (or increased value of the equity) of the company and what percentage ownership share each should have. Then you need to decide on the persons you want to have a say in the strategic operation of the business—they can sit on the board of directors, be general partners, or otherwise have a high-level voice in running the business. And finally, you need to choose a successor who will actively manage the business as its CEO, president, general partner, owner-manager, etc. Once these matters are decided, you need to prepare appropriate corporate documents, shareholder agreements, etc. that will put into effect your intentions. For this you will need the assistance of an experienced business attorney.

In choosing the persons who will oversee the business at a board of directors level, and especially in choosing the right person to manage the business, remember that the best choice for your family and other heirs is almost always the person who is the best person(s) to run the business, regardless of whether they are a member of your family.

If someone inside your family has the qualities and passion to manage your business, the respect of your employees and other key stakeholders, and the ability to take your business to greater heights, then by all means prepare that person to take over the reins when you are no longer able or no longer want to run the business. But putting a family member in charge of a business they are not prepared to lead does everyone a disservice, including the person who will be in over their head and get blamed when the family assets diminish on his or her watch. And in any event, if your family members who will own the enterprise going forward are not experienced in running the business, it may be a good idea to bring in some outside people to help plan and manage its operations.

In that respect, you should always have a strategic business plan in place that your successor understands inside and out. That way if anything unexpected happens to you, the business has the best chance of keeping a steady course during the transition period and beyond. It is also a good idea to make all key stakeholders aware of your succession plan. That way if there are any issues with who you have chosen as owners and managers for the future, they can be hashed out with you being involved in the process, and not on the fly during a period of turmoil due to your death or incapacity. The fewer surprises the better for all involved.

It is also a good idea to transition some or all the operations to your successor before a catastrophic event happens. It is always best for a new manager to learn the business gradually and already have assumed some operational control before he or she is thrown into the spotlight of leading the business. This will also help motivate your chosen successor to stay involved in the business and not jump to greener pastures as well.

Finally, your succession plan should also include a comprehensive top-to-bottom plan for keeping the business running successfully during the transition period. This means that your successor and other appropriate persons have all information necessary to run the business without you, including digital and hard copy information on assets, liabilities, bank accounts, lenders, customers, vendors, employees, contracts, etc. As such, it is a good idea for both business and estate planning purposes to make a list of all of your business assets, their function, and who has access to them, and make sure your successor has access to that list immediately upon your death or incapacity if not before.

Business Estate Planning Options

Once you know your plan for the future of your business, you can develop an estate plan that best maximizes the value of the business assets that are passed along at the time of your death and reflect your desires as to who will receive those assets. In doing so, you can refer to most of the options we have described in detail in the other chapters of this book. For the purposes of this section, we will point out some aspects of those options that are particular to transferring a business at the time of your death.

Will

If you are the sole owner of your business, you can transfer the assets or ownership interests of your business via a will, and if you are one of multiple owners, you can transfer your ownership interest using a will as well. Keep in mind, however, that these assets will have to go through probate, where the contents of your will are going to be publicly available. Probate will also cause a time delay before the new owners take legal title to these assets, which could cause significant problems for your business, particularly if the will is challenged. Finally, a will only allows you to transfer assets—you have no legally enforceable control of how they are used or managed afterwards.

Revocable Living Trust

For a business owner, a revocable living trust is most likely a better option than a will for passing along the business. This is true for many reasons, including:

- Allowing you to control the details not only of how your business assets are transferred, but how they are used and managed

- A trust does not go through probate, so the transfer is made quickly and privately

- The transfer is made without incurring probate costs

- Any appreciation in the value of the assets after they are transferred to the trust will not affect the size of your taxable estate

- You have flexibility in setting milestones for the transfer of assets held in the trust, and can appoint a successor trustee to manage the assets until your designated beneficiaries are old enough and capable enough to do so on their own

- You can combine aspects of a trust and a will by using a pour-over will, which states that all of your assets, including the ownership interest in a business, are to be distributed to a trust upon your death. Then the assets will be distributed as dictated by the trust agreement, which is a private document that need not be filed in court to be valid.

Gifts

A business owner can use the annual federal gift tax exclusion to give away ownership interests—such as shares of stock or limited partnership interests in the family business—each year on a tax-free basis. Ownership interests of greater value can be transferred tax-free up to the amount of the exclusion amount, but these gifts will reduce the amount of that credit available when you die. One additional benefit is that after a gift of an ownership interest is made, any appreciation in value will not affect your taxable estate.

Family Limited Partnership

You can create a limited partnership for which you are the general partner, and then contribute your business interests to the partnership or company and retain control of the business. You can then grant your chosen beneficiaries limited partnership interests, with whatever proportional interest in the partnership income that you decide. This transfer of assets to other members of your family can significantly reduce the size of your taxable estate. In addition, because the limited partnership interests are generally illiquid, the general partners can discount their value for gift tax purposes. The tax rules applicable to family limited partnerships are complex, however, so it is advisable to consult a professional in setting up and managing this type of entity.

Life Insurance and Irrevocable Life Insurance Trusts

One way to pay off business debts and estate taxes at the time of your death is to take out a life insurance policy on your life for that purpose. However, the proceeds of any life insurance policy will be included in your taxable estate. An Irrevocable Life Insurance Trust ("ILIT") is one of several ways to avoid this pitfall, because the ILIT is considered a separate entity for tax purposes. For you as the business owner, the life insurance will be on your life, and the trust will own the policy. Upon death, the life insurance policy will pay the trust and the proceeds will be tax-free.

Afterwards, the trust can use the proceeds to buy business assets from your estate, including the business itself, and thereby inject cash into the business and provide funds to pay estate taxes, funeral expenses, etc. The trust can then either continue to run the business on behalf of the beneficiaries, or it can sell the business without time pressure to pay taxes.

Estate Taxes

One of the biggest adverse effects of failing to create a business estate plan concerns estate tax. The interests you personally own in your business—e.g. assets in a sole proprietorship or shares of stock in a corporation—will become part of your taxable estate, and will be valued at the time you die. Because these assets can be very valuable but at the same time highly illiquid (difficult to sell and turn into cash), many persons inheriting a business find themselves in a position where they have to sell the business at much less than its fair market value just to pay the estate tax.

To avoid this, you should analyze all the options presented to you in this book for passing assets outside of the estate, including the use of trusts, assets with beneficiary designations, non-taxable gifts, family limited partnerships, etc. In addition, there are some estate planning options that are specific to a business, including "Section 303 stock redemptions" and "Section 6166 estate tax deferrals," each of which can be paid for by life insurance taken out on your life with the business as the beneficiary.

Section 303 of the Internal Revenue Code allows your estate to remove cash or other property from your business through a partial redemption of your stock. However, one requirement is that the value of the stock must be greater than 35 percent of the value of your estate. In addition, you can only take out enough to pay for your federal estate tax, state death taxes, funeral expenses, and administrative expenses.

Section 6166 of the Internal Revenue Code also is available if your business ownership constitutes more than 35 percent of your estate, provided you meet its other requirements. This section gives the executor the ability to elect to pay the estate tax attributable to the value of the business in 10 annual installments, beginning no later than five years after the date of your death.

In addition to these two provisions of the Internal Revenue Code, if your business qualifies as "family owned," you may be able to exclude part of it from estate taxation. Your business qualifies as family owned if the business comprises more than 50 percent of your total estate and you pass the estate on to a "qualified heir," meaning a spouse, child, grandchild or other descendent. However, your heirs must keep the business for at least 10 years following such an estate transfer.

Selection of Business Entity

Be aware that your business estate planning starts from the minute you select what type of legal entity your business will operate under. For example, the assets of a sole proprietorship are considered the assets of the owner. The owner's personal assets and the business assets are therefore lumped together to determine if any federal estate tax is due. This form of business ownership also exposes your entire estate to the creditors and liabilities of the business.

On the other hand, if you have properly formed and operated a corporation of some type, then its creditors should not be able to reach either your shares of stock in the corporation or your personal assets. However, if your shares of stock are going to pass by will or intestate, then the fair market value of that ownership interest at the time you die will be included in valuing your estate.

Business Valuation

No matter what type of business entity you select, you should determine the value of the business as part of your estate planning (keeping in mind the hopeful likelihood that the value of the business will appreciate over time). You first need to do so in order to estimate the value of your estate and plan accordingly with respect to the options you choose and the amount of cash your estate will need to pay estate taxes. In addition, your estate will need to report the valuation on your estate tax return, and if you are one of several owners and there is a buy-sell agreement in place, then the valuation will determine the price at which your ownership interest is purchased.

Multiple Owners

When a business has multiple owners, they will normally enter into a buy/sell agreement that lays out how to handle the shares of a deceased owner so they do not fall into the hands of an outside person who may have interests adverse to the business, or simply be disinterested or not qualified to participate in the business.

There are two main forms of buy-sell agreements: stock purchase and stock redemption. In an insurance-funded stock purchase arrangement, each business owner buys an insurance policy on the other, naming themselves as beneficiary. At the death of one of the owners, the surviving owners receive insurance proceeds to use in purchasing the deceased owner's stock from his or her estate.

In an insurance-funded stock-redemption arrangement, the corporation purchases the stock of a deceased shareholder. Here the business is the owner and beneficiary of life insurance policies on each shareholder.

It may also be the case that a combination of both is used, where the other owners have a right of first refusal on the deceased owner's shares, and if they do not purchase then the corporation can redeem the shares. An added benefit of having the share purchase funded by a life insurance policy is that the surviving family members can be assured they will receive enough cash in exchange for those shares. In addition, buy-sell agreements can also establish the value of the business for estate-tax purposes and ensure that your family gets a fair price for your ownership interest after the death of an owner.

CHAPTER 14

Digital Estate Planning

Preparing a Digital Estate Plan

Take a minute and think about how much of your life is performed and managed using a computer, a tablet, and/or a cell phone. The possibilities in today's technological age are vast: bank statements and account transactions; credit card statements, transactions and payments; investment accounts and transactions; e-mail accounts; social media such as Facebook and Twitter; digital storage facilities such as OneDrive and Amazon Cloud; etc. Now imagine what would happen if you unexpectedly died or became incapacitated. Even if you have taken the steps of naming a capable executor and/or trustee, and of granting a trusted person a durable power of attorney to manage your financial and personal affairs, do these persons have the information necessary to access your digital accounts? Would they know how to sort through the contents of these accounts even if they did have access information?

For example, do your executor, trustee and agent have access to a list of all your passwords to all your digital accounts? Do they have instructions on how to manage your digital accounts? If not, you could place them in an administrative and logistical nightmare attempting to unlock these accounts to perform their assigned tasks and protect your assets and estate. Bills could go unpaid, funds unmanaged, etc. until the person handling your affairs can produce the proper documents to the court and appropriate institutions that allows them the access and control, they need.

Therefore, in the modern age of digital technology, almost everyone's estate plan should include a plan for handling financial and social digital accounts. This digital estate plan should include:

- An inventory of digital assets and passwords

- Secure storage of passwords

- Selection of a digital guardian/executor

- Access to passwords

- Clear instructions on how to handle digital accounts

Making an Inventory of Digital Assets

You should create a detailed list of all your digital accounts, along with their passwords and security question answers. The importance of preparing and maintaining this inventory cannot be overstated, because it may be impossible for executors, other fiduciaries, and family members to discover many digital assets if they don't even know these assets exist and where to look for them. For security purposes, you may want to make two lists—one with the account numbers and one with the passwords and security question answers.

Your financial digital inventory should include the following:

- Bank accounts that you access online

- Brokerage accounts that you access online

- Retirement plan accounts that you access online

- Insurance plan accounts that you access online

- Credit card accounts that you access online

- Online retail accounts and digital wallet accounts

- Online sales accounts

- PayPal or other online payment accounts

- Utility bills and other services for which you pay online

- Tax information in digital form

- Business websites

- Business e-mail accounts

Your social digital inventory should include the following:

- Personal e-mail accounts
- Social media accounts such as Facebook, Twitter, and LinkedIn
- Data and document storage accounts like Drop-Box or Google Docs
- Personal websites
- Photo-sharing sites like Instagram or video-sharing sites like YouTube

In addition, you should inventory all your personal computers, laptop computers, tablets, and cell phones.

Make sure you update your digital inventory whenever you change an important password, and in any event as often as possible.

Safely Storing Digital Assets

Once you have created a digital inventory, the next step is to find a secure place to keep this vital information, which could lead to identity theft if obtained by the wrong person. Fortunately, new businesses are springing up to meet the modern digital challenges, including companies providing secure data storage. The key is to find a system that meets your strict security requirements and matches your technological capabilities to ensure that you use the system you select. One place not to put this information is in your will, because after you die this becomes a public document.

The options you do have for storing your digital account information and passwords include online storage accounts, password-protected electronic files, and old-fashioned methods such as a home safe.

Online Storage Accounts

Companies now offer services to allow users to store digital account information and passwords, as well as documents such as your wills and trusts, using state-of-the-art security for a monthly or yearly fee. Upon your death or incapacity, a person you designate is allowed immediate access to the online storage account and can obtain the digital information they need to manage your affairs. Remember, the information held in the online storage account must be accurate and up to date for the service to work as intended.

Currently popular online storage accounts include legacylocker.com and secureasafe.com. Do some research before choosing an online storage company. Most of these companies are new and therefore there is no guarantee that the one you choose will not go out of business. Also make sure their security and encryption systems are up to industry standards. Check that the connection between their system and your device is encrypted. This prevents interception while the data is being transmitted. Then be sure the data is also encrypted. No one should be able to unlock it without your password.

If you decide to use an online storage account to secure digital assets and information, you need to tell someone that the account exists. If you are not comfortable disclosing the existence of the online storage during your lifetime to the person who will have access upon your death or incapacity, then give the information to another fiduciary or very trusted family member or friend.

Password-protected Flash Drive or Computer File

You can keep your digital asset inventory on a USB flash drive or computer file, but to be secure the file in which the inventory resides should be encrypted with a complex password. The best way to do this is to use a software package designed to store confidential documents and passwords, such as KeePass, NordPass, or Web Confidential. The password to access the electronic list may be stored with original estate planning documents or in a safe-deposit box. Again, it is critical that this password be kept up to date. If a user changes the password and fails to replace the outdated password, the person designated to access the inventory will be unable to do so.

Old Fashioned Methods

If you are not comfortable with technology, or you trust an individual more than you trust online security systems, you can always do it the old-school way of putting your list in a fireproof home safe or safety deposit box at your bank. Or you can give a copy of the list to a trusted person like your spouse, child, best friend, or executor and make sure they keep it in a safe location as well. In any event, you need to guarantee someone knows the list exists, where it is located, and has the means to recover it.

Choosing a Digital Executor

Once you have created and stored your digital inventory, you need to select someone to have access to your digital accounts should you die or become incapacitated. This may well be the same person who is the executor of your entire estate, the trustee of your trusts, or the agent named in your general durable power of attorney. However, you need to make sure this person is technologically acute enough to handle the job of managing your digital assets, and if not find someone who is and name them as co-executor, co-trustee, or co-agent for the specific purpose of managing your digital estate. Then you need to provide this person with the access information and detailed instructions necessary to do so.

Instructions Regarding Your Digital Estate

While your estate plan should already describe what should happen to the assets contained in your digital accounts upon your death, you need to provide a road map to these accounts and specific instructions as to how to manage them, both to your executor and successor trustee upon your death, and any of your agents and alternate trustees upon your incapacity. This could be as simple as describing an automatic monthly credit card payment, or as complicated as a web of brokerage and investment accounts with supporting computer files.

In addition, you need to provide detailed instructions on how you want your e-mail accounts and social digital assets, such as Facebook and Twitter, handled. It is important that you review the terms and conditions of each of these accounts, because federal and state laws criminalize certain types of unauthorized access to computers or data. This means that if your executor or agent is not authorized to access one of your e-mail or other accounts under the provider's terms of service, then doing so could be a crime even if you expressly authorized access and provided the passwords.

Most social media services, including Facebook, Instagram, X, and LinkedIn, do not allow an assignment or transfer of a user's account. Therefore, your executor's choices for your social media accounts are to either request the deactivation or deletion of the account or leave the account as is.

CHAPTER 15

Finalizing Your Plan

Deciding What Should Be in Your Estate Plan

Now that you clearly understand the need for an estate plan, it is time to bring together all the pieces of the puzzle and create your plan. The types of estate planning tools that you use in your estate plan are largely dependent on your situation in life, your religious and philosophical views, and how you wish to distribute your assets. In most cases, assuming that your estate is not complex, you will most likely need only four or five documents to adequately prepare your estate. To complete these documents, you will need to consider your situation carefully and make important decisions in terms of what you want for the future.

We discuss some of these considerations briefly below.

Management of Your Property and Finances During Incapacity

One of the first issues that you will need to consider is whether you would like someone to manage your affairs during any period in which you are incapacitated or otherwise unable to do so yourself. If you make a positive decision in this respect, you will need to consider who would be best placed to act as your agent in the management of your property and finances. You will also need to consider whether any limitations should be placed on the scope of that person's authority.

Once you have determined what you want, the next step will be to create a durable power of attorney for finances and property.

Making Healthcare Decisions During Incapacity

In addition to having someone manage your financial affairs during a period of incapacity, you should also consider appointing one or more persons to make medical decisions for you during such a time. This appointment will be made under a healthcare power of attorney.

You should also consider whether you would like to set out any wishes in a living will regarding the end-of-life treatment that you would or would not like to receive should you ever find yourself in a state of permanent unconsciousness or suffering from a terminal illness. While some people find these decisions particularly difficult, they are nevertheless part and parcel of life and should be given due consideration as part of your overall estate plan.

Appoint Guardians for Your Children

If you have any children, you will need to consider who is best placed to care for them and manage their assets in your absence. Once you have determined who this person is or who these people are, as the case may be, you should ensure that you appoint them as guardians and property guardians of your children under the terms of your will. Remember to check with them first to make sure that they are willing to take on the role.

Assemble a List of Your Assets and Liabilities

When considering how you would like to deal with the distribution of your assets following your death, the first thing that you will need to do is to prepare an inventory of your assets and liabilities setting out the current net worth of each asset. This will enable you do determine the net value of your estate and therefore whether it falls within the scope of charges to estate tax.

If your estate is above the current tax threshold for estate tax, you will need to consider the use of methods to reduce your estate tax liabilities. These methods are set out in Chapter 11.

Your list of assets will also assist you in determining what assets you have to give away, to whom you would like to give them, and how you would like to give them away.

If the value of your assets is such that probate will be required, you should consider the use of a revocable living trust to help reduce the related probate fees.

In addition, the list should also help you determine what assets will need to be transferred into your revocable living trust and what assets you wish to leave under your will. Furthermore, it can be used to identify which accounts and policies should have the beneficiary designations changed so their proceeds and assets (in the case of broker accounts) will be distributed in accordance with your overall estate plan.

Decide Who Will Receive Your Assets

In conjunction with the preparation of your inventory of assets and liabilities, you can decide who you would like to give your assets to and who should receive those assets if the intended beneficiary passes away before you do or refuses the gift. Of course, you are generally free to leave your assets to anyone you choose. The major exception to this general rule relates to spouses. In all states, spouses have a legal entitlement to a percentage of their spouse's estate. In the absence of a spouse waiving this entitlement, you will need to make provision for them in your estate plan.

Decide How and When Your Beneficiaries Will Receive Your Assets

There are three principal ways in which you can leave assets to someone on your death: under a will; under a living trust; and by means of one of the non-probate transfer mechanisms referred to in Chapter 8. In using these methods, you can choose to leave your gifts directly to the beneficiary or to a trustee, custodian, or property guardian (for ease, we'll call each a "trustee" in this section) who will manage the gift on behalf of the beneficiary until they reach a certain age.

In deciding whether to make a gift to a beneficiary outright or to a trustee on their behalf, you will need to consider the age, health, and position in life of each of the proposed beneficiaries. If the gift is to a minor, it is wise to leave it in the care of a trustee. If you choose to do this, you will then need to consider whether you should establish a trust of your own either under your will or living trust or whether you simply utilize the trust provisions under your state's Uniform Transfers to Minors Act (UTMA). Alternatively, you could simply leave the assets to their guardian who will determine how best to manage the proceeds on their behalf.

Similarly, if you have decided to make a gift to an incapacitated person, you will need to consider how that gift will be managed on their behalf. It may well be the case that the person in question has a guardian or agent who can manage that gift but, if not, you may wish to consider setting up a trust fund for them. Where trust funds are established, you will need to determine how long it should continue for and what will happen to the assets in the trust fund if the intended beneficiary dies before they receive the benefit of the trust. In this respect, you should consider nominating alternate beneficiaries unless you want the assets to be passed to the person or persons entitled to the residuary estate.

Choosing People to Be in Charge

Apart from leaving your assets to loved ones after you pass, estate planning is fundamentally about choosing the right people to deal with your affairs when you are unable to do so or no longer around to do so. It follows, therefore, that in putting an estate plan together you need to carefully select people to act as executors, successor trustees, trustees, guardians, healthcare agents, agents under a power of attorney and agents under a living will. The selection of the right people will be fundamental to the overall success of your estate plan. We mention in this book several different attributes that you should look for in selecting these people and you should refer to these in making your decisions.

Resource

If you decide to prepare your own estate planning documents, we recommend using "Will Writer," EstateBee's estate planning software.

EstateBee's unique software will, through a question and answer process, guide you through the process of preparing a variety of estate planning documents including wills, living trusts, powers of attorneys, living wills and more.

To learn more about this software, see the information pages at the back of this book or visit **www.estate-bee.com.**

When to 'Do-It-Yourself' and When to Include Lawyers

The next step is to decide whether you need to visit your attorney or whether you wish to prepare an estate plan yourself. Both have their own unique advantages.

Your attorney should be able to advise you as to how you can best accomplish your objectives. He or she may force you to think about the choices that you have made or may even present you with better alternatives. Engaging an attorney to review your personal situation and assist with the preparation of an estate plan is often the best way to ensure that the goals set out in your estate plan are achieved. However, the legal fees incurred in the preparation of an estate plan can be quite significant. It is for this reason alone that many people decide to prepare their own estate plans using books such as this one.

Unless your estate or situation is complex (i.e. it consists of complicated asset ownership structures or has potential estate tax exposures), there is no real reason why you cannot prepare your own estate planning documents. This is particularly so if you wish to keep matters straightforward and easily understood. If this is the case, there is no reason why you cannot prepare your own will, living trust, power of attorney, living will, etc. All that is necessary is a little diligent research into the laws applicable in your state. And with the assistance of this book, and some of the other products from the EstateBee estate planning range, there is no reason why you cannot confidently deal with these matters yourself. However, if you do not feel comfortable making your own estate plan, it is best that you contact an attorney.

Storing Your Documents

Once you have prepared your documents, you will need to consider how and where you should store them. While there are several options available to you, the principal requirement is that you store them in a safe and accessible place where they can be accessed when needed.

In fact, when it comes to storing legal documents, many people's first choice is to use a safe deposit box. While this is a logical choice when it comes to safety, it is not always practical. In many states if the box is registered solely in your name, then on your death it will be automatically sealed and your family will need to obtain a court order to open it and remove it contents—that's if they know about it at all. Similar problems arise in times of incapacity. Again, your family may not be able to access your living trust, power of attorney or living will documents.

For these reasons, it may be useful to consider having a safe deposit registered in the joint names of you and someone else. This someone else can be a spouse or indeed an executor, successor trustee or agent under a power of attorney or AMD. In this way, at least someone will be able to access the safe deposit box both in times of your incapacity and on your death.

If the idea of registering a safe deposit box in joint names does not appeal to you for privacy or other reasons, there are several other options available to you. The key criteria will be safety. Make sure to choose a location where the documents will be protected from both fire and flooding. Ideally, you could use a personal safe located either at home or in your office. Always ensure that someone knows the location of your safe and indeed the fact that the documents have been placed in it. Be sure, however, to consider the privacy and security issues associated with letting a person know the combination of your safe or the details of how they can find out that combination.

Alternatively, you could consider asking your attorney to store your documents for safekeeping or you could just keep them in a safe place in your home. The choice is yours. Wherever you decide to keep them, it is a good practice to keep copies of these documents where they can be located so that your estate plan can be recreated if it ever needs to be.

Updating Your Estate Plan

It is important to update your estate plan regularly. In fact, we recommend that you update it at least every two to three years or whenever there is a significant change in your personal circumstances. By significant change, we mean the occurrence of events such as marriage, divorce, the birth of a child, adoption, or a relevant change in either state law or tax law. You should also consider updating your plan where there has been a significant change to your financial position.

Over time, you will probably change your mind as to whom you wish your assets to pass. At times, the beneficiaries under your estate plan may predecease you, as might your executors and trustees, or you may dispose of assets and acquire new ones. All these matters should force you to reconsider the terms of your estate plan and whether the estate plan needs to be updated.

In addition, as most states afford spouses a right to claim a particular share of their spouse's estate, a material change in your financial position could result in your estate plan no longer meeting those requirements. As such, you will need to re-visit the provisions of your estate plan to ensure that state law does not intervene to determine how your assets are distributed. This might result in the unfortunate circumstance that some of your named beneficiaries might not receive the assets you wished to gift to them.

Every time you update your estate plan you should consider your overall objective and then each aspect of your plan to ensure that it meets that overall objective. Maybe you would prefer to name new executors or healthcare agents? Maybe minor beneficiaries have now grown up and the use of trusts is no longer appropriate? Maybe your adult children have difficulty managing money and it is more prudent to place their inheritance under the management of a trustee rather than giving it to them outright? Be sure that you carefully consider your whole estate plan and not just part of it—remember that every aspect of your plan interacts with every other part.

Finally....

We wish you well in preparing your estate plan. For further information and tools to assist you in the preparation of your plan, we recommend that you visit www.estate-bee.com.

Appendices

Appendix 1

Estate Planning Worksheet

Downloadable Worksheet

Blank copies of the worksheet contained in this kit can be downloaded from the EstateBee website. Simply login to your account or, if you don't have an account, you can create one for free.

www.estate-bee.com/login

Once logged in, go to your profile page and enter the code listed below in the 'Use Codes' tab:

EPEWORK2020

Estate Planning Worksheet

Estate *Bee*

www.estate-bee.com

Estate Planning Worksheet

Before you begin the process of creating an estate plan, we recommend that you print out this worksheet and complete it as appropriate. It will help you to work out what assets you actually own, and identify your liabilities, before deciding who you would like to make gifts to and how. By having all the relevant details at your fingertips it will save a considerable amount of time in the preparation of your estate planning documents.

The document is also useful for document your choice of fiduciaries such as executors, trustees, and healthcare agents.

In addition, by keeping this worksheet with your will and other personal papers, it will greatly assist your executor in identifying and locating your assets and liabilities when the time comes.

Personal Information	You	Your Spouse
Full Name:		
Birth Date:		
Social Security Number:		
Occupation:		
Work Telephone:		
Work Fax:		
Mobile/Pager:		
Email Address:		
Home Address (Include County):		
Home Telephone:		
Home Fax:		

Date and Place of Marriage:	
Maiden name of Spouse:	
If either of you were previously married, list the dates of prior marriage, name of previous spouse, names of living children from prior marriage(s), and state whether marriage ended by death or divorce:	
Location of Safe Deposit Box (if any):	

Notification of Death

(On my death, please notify the following persons)

Full Name	Telephone	Address

Children (Living)		
Full Name	Address (if the child does not reside with you)	Birth Date
Children (Deceased)		
Full Name		
Grandchildren		
Full Name	Address	Birth Date

Parents

Full Name	Address	Telephone Number

Brothers and Sisters

Full Name	Address	Telephone Number

Assets

Description & Location	Current Fair Market Value	How is Title Held?
Real Estate (Land and Buildings)		

Closely Held Companies, Businesses, Partnerships etc.		
Bank Accounts		
Shares, Bonds and Mutual Funds		
Vehicles, Boats, etc		

Other Property		
Total		

Liabilities

Description	Amount
Mortgages	
Loans	

Debts	
Other Liabilities	
Total	

Life Insurance and Annuities

Company	Insured	Beneficiary(ies)	Face Amount	Cash Value
Total				

Pensions and Other Retirement Plans

Company Custodian	Participant	Type of Plan	Vested Amount	Death Benefit
Total				

Distribution Plan
(Describe in general terms how you wish to leave your property at death)

Other Beneficiaries

(Information about persons other than your spouse and family members who you wish to benefit)

Full Name	Age	Address	Relationship to You

Fiduciaries

(List name, address and home telephone for each person)

	Full Name	Address	Telephone Number
Last Will and Testament			
Primary Executor:			
First Alternate Executor:			
Second Alternate Executor:			

Primary Trustee:			
First Alternate Trustee:			
Second Alternate Trustee:			
Guardian of Minor Children:			
First Alternate Guardian:			
Second Alternate Guardian:			
Living Trust			
Successor Trustee:			
First Alternate Successor Trustee:			
Second Alternate Successor Trustee:			
Agent under a Power of Attorney for Finance and Property			
Agent:			
First Alternate Agent:			
Second Alternate Agent:			
Agent under a Healthcare Power of Attorney			
Healthcare Agent:			

First Alternate Healthcare Agent:			
Second Alternate Healthcare Agent:			
Living Will			
Healthcare Agent:			
First Alternate Healthcare Agent:			
Second Alternate Healthcare Agent:			

Advisors

(List name, address and home telephone for each person)

	Full Name	Address	Telephone Number
Lawyer			
Accountant			
Financial Advisor			
Stockbroker			
Insurance Agent			
Other Information:			

Document Locations		
Description	Location	Other Information
Last Will & Testament		
Trust Agreement		
Living Will		
Healthcare Power of Attorney		
Power of Attorney for Finance and Property		
Title Deeds		
Leases		
Share Certificates		
Mortgage Documents		
Birth Certificate		
Marriage Certificate		
Divorce Decree		
Donor Cards		

Other Documents	

Funeral Plan

(Describe in general terms what funeral and burial arrangements you would like to have)

EstateBee's Estate Planning Range

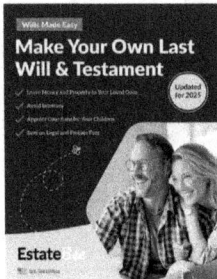

Make Your Own
Last Will & Testament

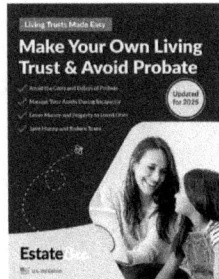

Make Your Own
Living Trust & Avoid
Probate

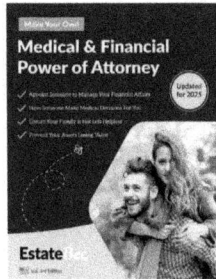

Make Your Own
Medical & Financial
Power of Attorney

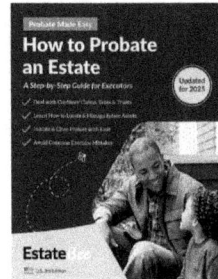

How to Probate an
Estate - A Step-by-Step
Guide for Executors

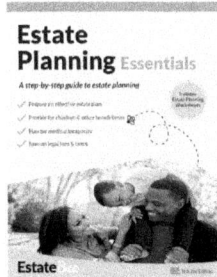

Estate Planning
Essentials - A Step-by-
Step Guide to Estate
Planning

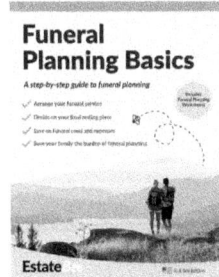

Funeral Planning Basics
– A Step-by-Step Guide
to Funeral Planning

Legal Will Kit

Living Trust Kit

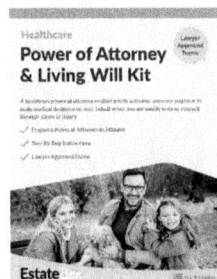

Healthcare Power of
Attorney & Living
Will Kit

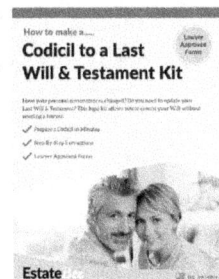

Codicil to a Last
Will & Testament Kit

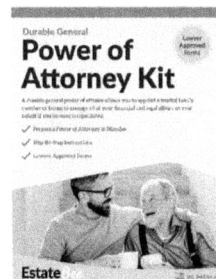

Durable General
Power of Attorney Kit

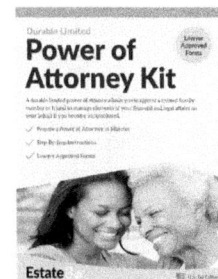

Durable Limited
Power of Attorney Kit

www.ingramcontent.com/pod-product-compliance
Lightning Source LLC
Chambersburg PA
CBHW051209200326
41519CB00025B/7051